You Can't Do That To Me!

Jules Archer

YOU CAN'T DO THAT TO ME!

Famous Fights for Human Rights

MACMILLAN PUBLISHING CO., INC.
New York
COLLIER MACMILLAN PUBLISHERS
London

Macmillan Publishing Co., Inc.
866 Third Avenue, New York, N.Y. 10022
Collier Macmillan Canada, Ltd.
Printed in the United States of America

10 9 8 7 6 5 4 3 2 1

LIBRARY OF CONGRESS CATALOGING IN PUBLICATION DATA
Archer, Jules.   You can't do that to me.
Bibliography: p.   Includes index.
SUMMARY: A history of the struggle for human rights,
from ancient times to the present.
1. Civil rights—History—Juvenile literature.
[1. Civil rights—History] I. Title.
JC571.A68 1980   323.4'09   79-5127   ISBN 0–02–705600–7

For my grandchildren
Zachary, Kirsten, Rory, Ryan and Nathaniel Archer
who will always, i hope,
enjoy their human rights

CONTENTS

You Can't Do That To Me!

INTRODUCTION

From the days of Israelites suffering under the Pharaoh to the oppression of Chileans under the tyrannical Pinochet, men and women have cried out, "You can't do that to me!" But power is so intoxicating that those who wield it often show cruel disregard for the lives, liberty, and well-being of those they govern.

Human rights, as citizens of the United States understand them, are the guarantees of personal freedom and safety spelled out in our Constitution and Bill of Rights. Not all the world's governments agree with this concept. The Soviet Union, for example, denies civil liberties to the Russian people.

On the other hand, it guarantees its citizens the right to a job, a low-cost dwelling, and free medical care. These economic rights, the Soviet government insists, are far more important human rights than civil liberties.

Most people would prefer to have both types of human rights. But when forced to choose, they invariably prefer to live protected by laws, under a government that cannot persecute or torture them or jail or execute them unjustly.

How strongly the democratic nations of the world feel about civil liberties was emphasized in 1977 by the award of the Nobel Peace Prize to Amnesty International (AI), an organization that works for the release of individuals around the world imprisoned for their political or religious convictions.

Founded in London in 1961, AI now has more than 100,000 members in seventy-eight countries. They investigate the persecution of peaceful dissidents by imprisonment and torture, a practice they have found to be government policy in over sixty countries. Pressing the cases of over 15,000 political prisoners from 1971 through 1980, AI has won the release of more than half.

"Its efforts on behalf of defending human dignity against violence and subjugation," said the Nobel committee, "have proved that the basis for peace in the world must be justice for all human beings."

Citizens denied their human rights usually live under an undemocratic government, whether of the extreme right or left. Both anti-Communist and Communist regimes insist that repressive measures are necessary for "national security," to prevent revolutionary (or counterrevolutionary) activities by "enemies of the state." Critics and political opponents are frequently imprisoned as "subversives."

When Jimmy Carter became president, the United States' prestige as a moral power in the world had been badly damaged by its involvement in the Vietnam war and by the Watergate scandal. Carter sought to rekindle world respect for the United States by speaking out in support of human rights everywhere.

It was his intention, the president said, "to weave a due regard for those rights into the fabric" of United States foreign policy. He wrote an open letter of encouragement to leading Russian dissident Andrei Sakharov, and reminded Soviet leader Leonid Brezhnev that the Russians had signed an agreement at Helsinki to respect human rights.

Brezhnev expressed indignation at Carter's "interference" in the internal affairs of the Soviet Union. The State Department grew concerned that the Soviet-American détente might be broken and that the Russians might refuse to sign an American-initiated nuclear arms control agreement. President Carter gradually fell silent about Communist shortcomings. To indicate that he was not singling out the Soviet Union alone for rebuke, Carter also criticized the brutal right-wing South American military dictatorships in Chile, Brazil, Paraguay and Uruguay.

Carter also indicated that the United States' foreign policy would no longer give full aid and support to such dictatorships, unless they began restoring civil liberties to their people.

"He is giving not just Americans but people in the West generally," said Anthony Lewis in the *New York Times*, "a sense that their values are being asserted again, after years of silence in the face of tyranny and brutality."

The issue of human rights dominated the world press.

"One of the incidental effects of this necessarily somewhat experimental effort," Carter observed, "has been a nationwide—indeed worldwide—debate on the nature of human rights and how best they may be advanced." He warned that no "quick or easy" results could be expected in a struggle which had been going on for centuries. "History moves slowly and fitfully," he declared. "But as long as we are true to ourselves, history, where human rights are concerned, is on our side."

In this book I have tried to describe some of this history. Selecting milestones on the long, winding road toward individual freedom, I have omitted very familiar examples, such as the American and French revolutions. I have selected other illustrations of the human spirit that challenges tyranny by crying out defiantly, "You can't do that to me!"

People who join the struggle for human rights don't always win. Sometimes they succeed for a period, only to be cast down once more, like the Chileans who won human rights under President Salvador Allende, but lost them again when a military coup overthrew the Allende regime.

Sometimes people lose them for a period only to regain them, as happened in India when Prime Minister Indira Gandhi suspended democracy in 1975 and jailed over 100,000 political opponents. When she finally allowed elections, the people rose and voted her out of office. She made a comeback as prime minister in 1980 because of India's economic difficulties, but indicated that this time she would not suspend the Indian constitution.

People who struggle for human rights sometimes win them permanently, as did the Sinn Fein movement against British rule in southern Ireland. Or their struggle may win only a limited goal, but pave the way for full freedom later—as did the Mazzini-Garibaldi movement in nineteenth-century Italy.

Sometimes the fight for human rights is a mass movement, like the Peasants' Revolt in fourteenth-century England, the Danish underground struggle against Nazi occupation during World War II, the centuries-old fight of the Basques for independence from Spain, and the struggle of Afghan patriots against the Soviet invasion of their country in 1980.

The crusade may also be waged by only a handful of dedicated rebels, as in the barons' revolt against King John in 1215, the Risorgimento revolts in nineteenth-century Italy, the South American rebellions organized by Simon Bolivar, and the present struggle of Russian dissidents against the Kremlin.

Sometimes a few brave persons' struggle for human rights arouses and inspires vast numbers of the oppressed to unite behind them. This occurred in the slave revolt led by Spartacus in ancient Rome; the 1922 general strike in China; and the struggle of Jomo Kenyatta against British colonialism in Kenya.

To be successful, Mao Tse-tung has pointed out, "revolutionaries must swim in the sea of the people." A handful of revolutionaries who seize power from an oppressive regime in a coup d'état may in turn be corrupted by power, unless they turn it over to the people's elected representatives.

The struggles for human rights all over the globe must concern us all. The United States State Department expressed concern in 1978 over the treatment of Arabs in Israeli-held territory, stating, "Documented reports of the use of extreme physical and psychological pressures during interrogations, and instances of brutality by individual interrogators cannot be ruled out."

Israeli authorities also invaded Palestinian homes seeking terrorist suspects and literature, expelled Palestinian leaders from the West Bank, and seized large tracts of Arab land. Such oppressive acts can only provoke fresh Arab terrorism and possibly escalate into a Middle Eastern war that would affect us all.

Injustice in the Republic of South Africa could touch off a continental race war that could upset relations between black and white people all over the world. Injustice in the Soviet Union, as well as its invasion of Afghanistan, has already strained Soviet-American relations and could end détente, forcing us to worry once more about the threat of nuclear war.

We *are* our brother's keeper, of necessity, if not out of conscience. We also have a moral obligation to preserve our domestic human rights, won by the twenty-year struggle of our founding fathers from 1763 to 1787. If we are to pass these rights to our children and grandchildren, we cannot permit any administration to curb or cancel them in the name of national security.

We must say no to government attempts to wiretap our phones at will, no to searches of homes without a court warrant, no to arrests made without regard to due process of law, no to censorship of what we read or see, no to suppression of any unpopular viewpoint, no to the denial to some citizens of rights accorded others.

If instead we let civil liberties be violated, our democracy will vanish along with our human rights.

The struggles described in this book reveal how difficult it is for a people to win human rights or to regain them once they have been lost. We must never become complacent and take our human rights for granted. We must stand prepared to join together to fight every attempt to weaken these rights or take them away.

"Eternal vigilance," said Irish statesman John Philpot Curran in 1790, "is the price of liberty."

Jules Archer

1

NOTHING TO LOSE
BUT YOUR CHAINS

The Revolt of Spartacus

On a sunny day in 73 B.C. the great square at Capua, just north of Naples, swarmed with slave dealers and their merchandise. One slave in particular stood out, made conspicuous by the felt *caveat emptor* cap on his head which warned buyers that he came with no guarantee of docility. The purchaser should not expect his money to be refunded if this slave ran away, or committed murder or suicide. The slave's name: Spartacus.

The chalk that whitened his feet indicated that he was an imported slave, a prisoner of war. A scroll around his neck informed prospective buyers that he had been the son of a nomadic chief in Thrace, a land now merged into eastern Greece and western Turkey.

The only buyers who bid on Spartacus were promoters. These men hired out troupes of gladiators to kill one another or to fight wild animals for entertainment at private banquets or public arenas. The highest bidder was a Capuan promoter, who had Spartacus branded as his personal property.

The new gladiator was then given a pair of the barbarian

trousers worn by all slaves taken in war, along with a simple gray tunic and a pair of wooden shoes. Placed in shackles, he was marched off chained to other slaves from Thrace and Gaul, bought criminals and captured army deserters.

The demand for gladiators was greatest in Rome and Capua, the second great city of the Roman Republic. Wealthy patricians, members of the ruling class, vied with each other in giving lavish banquets and entertainments to mark funeral rites, weddings, and army victories. Even more importantly, gladiators were used to woo public favor. Candidates for public office sought votes by trying to present the bloodiest slave fights in Roman arenas.

Such spectacles were also used by the ruling class of Rome to keep free workers pacified. The aristocrats lived in great luxury, their riches amassed by slaves toiling in their factories, fields, and mines. The ever-increasing use of slaves made it impossible for the majority of free workers to demand a living wage. But slaves worked primarily in manual labor which Roman free workers considered beneath them.

Spartacus's new home was a large building with tiny cells surrounding a central courtyard. The gladiator school contained a prison in which reluctant combatants were placed in leg irons and shackles and whipped and burned with hot irons. Tiny punishment cells, without enough room for a man to sit up, stand, or lie flat, held half-dead gladiators who had tried to escape.

The school was operated for the promoter by a trainer, or *lanista*, Lentulus Batiates. The ex-gladiator kept trainees under heavy guard night and day, not only to thwart escape attempts but also to prevent suicides. Some desperate slaves considered suicide preferable to the agonies of death in the arena. One gladiator placed his neck under a heavy moving cart. Another cut his wrists with shards from his smashed drinking bowl. A third impaled himself on a guard's sword during training exercises.

Spartacus was led to a dark bare cell. A stone shelf, covered by a straw-filled mattress, served as a bed. Every day Spartacus worked out in the courtyard for grueling hours of combat practice. As a Thracian he was given a round wooden buckler, or shield, and dagger. Samnites were given a shield and sword. Other slaves fought with nets and tridents.

Matched against each other in practice bouts, the slaves fought until someone was wounded. Any gladiator who hesitated or showed fear was lashed, or hung by his arms with weights attached to his feet and then flogged. Stubborn failure to demonstrate fighting spirit brought transfer to a quarry, where an overseer's whip would compel backbreaking labor from dawn till dusk. Any gladiator or slave who dared attack his master or an overseer, or who took part in a revolt, paid an automatic price—crucifixion.

Like most slaves imprisoned at the gladiator school, Spartacus dreamed of escape. But the attempt was dangerous. Recaptured runaways were tortured, then branded on the forehead with the letter F for *fugitivus* ("fugitive"). Metal collars were riveted around their necks offering a reward for their apprehension if they escaped.

Spartacus was forced to swear the gladiator's oath "to suffer myself to be whipped with rods, burned with fire or killed with steel if I disobey."

Spartacus's first trial by combat came when a wealthy contractor wanted six slaves to fight in his private arena for the amusement of his guests. Spartacus and two other Thracian gladiators fought against three captured German prisoners of war from another training school. One Thracian and two Germans were slain. Spartacus was filled with revulsion at having been forced to kill a man for the amusement of a few patricians.

He subsequently fought in both public and private arenas. Once he was part of an entertainment in which several hundred gladiators fought in a wild free-for-all. The object of this event was to survive for two hours. Fighting bravely and coolly, Spartacus tried to kill as few gladiators as possible without endangering his own life.

Spartacus was quick on his feet and managed to survive six months of combat without serious wounds; he suffered only a crushed nose and minor injuries. His hatred of the Romans became increasingly bitter. Spartacus lived in constant dread that each day would be his last. If he was lucky, he escaped being selected to fight at a scheduled event. But he could not avoid sickening reminders of tomorrow, as dead or badly injured gladiators were carried back from arenas.

In desperation Spartacus began spreading a subversive idea among his fellow gladiators. Why, he whispered, should gladiators kill each other for the Romans' entertainment? There was nothing in Capua for them but eventual death. Why not agree to revolt at a given signal, sweep aside Lentulus and his *lanistae*, and escape? Then each slave could bolt for his own native land.

Spartacus was careful about those he approached. He chose only those gladiators he knew hated their Roman masters fiercely. His judgment was sound. None betrayed him to Lentulus for personal gain.

Two Celtic gladiators, Crixus and Oenomaus, became his lieutenants in the plan. The conspiracy spread rapidly until 200 gladiators had joined, eager for any chance of freedom, even at the risk of crucifixion.

Before Spartacus could set a date for the revolt, a *lanista* overheard two gladiators whispering about the plot. He reported it at once to Lentulus. The two gladiators and others in nearby cells were tortured for information. Spartacus knew he dared not wait a moment longer.

Crixus and Oenomaus passed the word: *"Now!"*

The three leaders hastily gathered some sixty gladiators and led them in a lightning raid on the school's kitchen. The few *lanistae* who tried to stop them with whips and knives were quickly overpowered. The gladiators seized every possible weapon in the kitchen—chopping knives, spits, roasting forks, cleavers, pestles, blocks of firewood. Pot covers were snatched for use as shields.

Most of the slaves in the kitchen were women. They joined the revolt, bringing the number of rebels to seventy-four. Spartacus and his followers decided to crash out of the school through the bolted wooden doors of the kitchen.

Two *lanistae*, whirling knotted whips, tried to hold them off and called for help to a maniple of Roman soldiers on guard outside the training school. But before the troops could break into the courtyard and put down the rebellion, the *lanistae* were swept aside. Smashing the bolts on the doors, the gladiators burst out of the building.

Freedom! Spartacus and his small rebel army had little time to rejoice. The Roman maniple quickly formed ranks in the square, then charged with swords and spears. The gladiators outnumbered the soldiers and were fierce fighters. But Spartacus knew that kitchen weapons were no match for heavy armor.

He ordered his followers to disperse in a wide circle and fire rocks at the soldiers. As the slaves scattered, the Roman troops were left without a concentrated target. Splitting up to chase the rebels, many soldiers went down under a hail of stones or were assaulted from behind.

The gladiators, expert at dodging and twisting in the arena, suffered only a few casualties. The maniple lost heavily and its remnants finally fled.

Spartacus and his followers stripped the dead of their spears and swords. Racing through the city, they came upon several wagons transporting weapons for arena spectacles. They overpowered the drivers and armed themselves fully, throwing away their kitchen weapons.

When a second maniple of Roman soldiers challenged them, Spartacus and his rebels stood their ground and fought off the troops. Although he had ordered the women to the rear, Spartacus discovered that they had taken part in the battle by throwing rocks at the Romans.

The rebels rejoiced at their successful escape. But now where could they go? It was one thing to break out of a gladiators' school and fight off two maniples of home guards. It would be another to stand up to the powerful force of Roman centurions that would undoubtedly be sent to hunt them down.

The rebels needed a place to hide until they could organize a plan of escape to their homes overseas. Crixus knew the region well and had a suggestion. Mount Vesuvius would make a perfect refuge. Even if the Romans discovered where they were, the fugitives would be shielded by the natural fortress of the volcano's cave. It was accessible only by one narrow and difficult passage which would be impregnable if kept under guard by the gladiators.

Spartacus led his forces south toward Vesuvius.

Meanwhile, news of the gladiators' escape had spread panic among the Roman citizenry from Neapolis to Rome, especially among the patricians. Nothing was more dreaded than a slave uprising. Aristocrats worried that the poor might join a slave uprising and sweep aside the whole oppressive structure of Roman society.

"Every slave we own," the Roman saying went, "is an enemy we harbor." Now, with Spartacus and his companions loose in the countryside, patricians feared that their great estates would be seized and looted, Roman noblewomen kidnapped and raped.

Spartacus's little band grew steadily. Field slaves fled from farms to join the gladiators, bringing hoes and other farm implements as weapons. The government in Rome announced large rewards for the capture of the "criminals" who had stolen themselves.

A force of 3,000 Romans under Gaius Claudius Pulcher encamped at the base of Vesuvius, blockading the narrow entrance. Pulcher intended to starve the slave army into surrender. Vesuvius's outer walls were steep and slippery. If the rebels tried to break out by descending them, they would plunge to their deaths.

Spartacus and his lieutenants debated how to escape the trap. Oenomaus argued passionately that it would be better to die fighting as free men. If they did not challenge Pulcher for the passageway, killing as many Romans as they could, they would surely die a lingering death by starvation. Crixus argued for negotiating with Pulcher for surrender on condition that they would not be crucified, and that the women rebels would not be punished.

But Spartacus had a third plan. Wild vines growing around the top of the volcano had given him an idea. He ordered his men to gather and twist the vines together into long thick rope. On a dark night, with a strong gladiator stationed at the crest of the rear cliff to anchor the rope, one by one the slaves slid down to the outside base of the volcano.

When the last rebel had gone, the gladiator rested and waited for his own liberation.

Spartacus and his little army slipped silently around the base of Vesuvius, single file. They surrounded the rear of Pulcher's camp. Except for a few soldiers on guard duty, the Roman troops were asleep. The gladiators seized the guards from behind, cutting their throats. Then they fell upon Pulcher and his men. Over a thousand Romans died in the first moments of the attack. The rest fled in panic.

News of the slave army's new victory reverberated throughout the Roman republic. Hundreds of slaves, joined by prisoners who escaped from the workhouses, swarmed to Spartacus, who armed them with Roman weapons.

Wary of being trapped again inside Vesuvius, the rebels swept out onto the plains, encamping like a regular army. The Roman praetor, Publius Varinius, took the field against them with powerful forces. Reaching the slaves' reported encampment, he found them gone. To Varinius's dismay, Spartacus and his men circled around the marching Romans and attacked their rear guard of 2,000 men. In the confusion, Varinius was forced to order a retreat.

The jubilant gladiators shouted and hugged each other in triumph. Slaves were defeating the powerful Roman army again and again! Spartacus was swept up in the general euphoria. Before, the plan to fight their way back to their homes had been just an aspiration. Now, for the first time, he had real hope that they could battle their way through Italy to the Alps and from there scatter back to their own lands.

He led his army from plantation to plantation, freeing slaves along the way and adding them to his followers. Each time the Romans sent soldiers against them, the rebels were stronger. There were greater numbers, and they had more good weapons which they had wrested from their attackers.

Spartacus's strategy inspired the slave soldiers. They were fighting for more than their own liberty. Now they were also liberating thousands and thousands of oppressed slaves as they fought their way to freedom. If enough slaves joined them, who would be left to till the soil or work in the factories? The Roman republic might even collapse.

Then, perhaps, a new world order would be born, one in which everyone would be entitled to human rights.

The spectacular conflict, known as the Slave or Gladiators' War, grew. Reverberations spread swiftly like ripples from a stone splashing in a pond. Slave uprisings began to erupt in distant parts of the Roman world. More escaped slaves came over hills and across valleys to join Spartacus.

His army became a formidable fighting force. Many of the deserting slaves were Celtic and Teutonic prisoners of war, brave and experienced fighting men. Moving up and down the Apennines, the rebels plundered towns in the plains. Roman troops sent against them were defeated. For two years the slave army terrorized the whole Italian peninsula.

The sins of the slave owners returned to haunt them. The slaves showed no more mercy than had been shown to them in bondage. Many patricians were crucified, as rebellious slaves had been. Gladiators took revenge by forcing captured Roman nobles to slaughter each other in gladiatorial combat, for the rebels' amusement.

Sweeping aside two Roman forces sent to stop him, Spartacus marched his army northward to the Alps. He told his army that they must escape before their triumphs turned to ashes.

But the victorious slaves were intoxicated by their seeming invincibility. Now more than just free men, they were masters of the great Roman republic! Spartacus's lieutenant, Crixus, warned him that if he insisted upon crossing the Alps, much of their army would desert. In 71 B.C. under pressure from his other lieutenant, Oenomaus, Spartacus reluctantly agreed to turn and march on Rome instead.

As the slave army approached, consternation reigned in the capital of the republic. Some home forces—ordinary citizens known as plebians—drafted by Roman praetor Marius Licinius Crassus refused to fight. They balked at being used as pawns to pull patrician chestnuts out of the fire. What did it profit plebians to die fighting slaves in order to preserve a patrician-controlled society?

"Wild beasts have their lairs, but the men who fight and die for Italy can call nothing their own except the air and the sunshine," one tribune—a spokesman for the people—told them. He added, "Your generals exhort you to fight for hearth and home. . . . You have neither. . . . You fight to defend the luxury of the rich. They call you the masters of the world but you have not a foot of land you can call your own!"

When 500 soldiers of Crassus's army threw away their weapons and fled, he pursued them and forced them to hold a deadly lottery. The "winners"—one man in ten—were executed, according to the ancient Roman practice of decimation. With a fear of authority restored by this harsh punishment, Crassus led his chastened legion against Spartacus.

The Roman Senate hastily summoned two of Rome's ablest generals—Lucullus in Thrace and Pompey in Spain—to return at once with their legions. The Slave War had to be won quickly before the whole system of Roman slavery was subverted.

Meanwhile Crassus beat the slave army back from the approaches to Rome, and pursued it to the peninsula of Bruttium. Bottling up Spartacus and his men, Crassus built a thirty-two-mile ditch and wall across the neck of the peninsula, and encamped to wait until the slave army was starved into surrender.

Spartacus waited for a dark, snowy night, then ordered his men to fill in—as quietly as possible—a section of the ditch with earth and tree boughs. Storming over the wall at this point, Spartacus and his men were able to break through and escape before Crassus's surprised legions could recover and reseal the exit.

But the slaves refused to retreat, insisting that Spartacus commit their entire army to a showdown with Crassus's forces, a battle that would decide once and for all whether they would remain slave or free.

Spartacus pleaded with them for prudence, but his chief lieutenants, Crixus and Oenomaus, sided against him. With heavy heart, Spartacus led the rebels out of the mountains and down into the plains.

Crassus, delighted, formed his legions. His army vastly outnumbered Spartacus's forces, which fought best in guerrilla warfare. Crassus was hungry for a quick and total victory. Otherwise, Pompey would arrive with his legions and steal all the glory for himself!

The rival forces took their positions on the battlefield. When Spartacus's horse was brought to him, he refused to mount it. Instead he drew his sword and slew the beast.

"If we win the day," he told Crixus and Oenomaus, "I will have my choice of a great many better horses. If we lose the day, I will have no further need of this beast as I shall not live to ride it again."

On foot, Spartacus led his slave army toward Crassus's vast cohorts. The Romans were drawn up in the order of battle, with 2,400 cavalry in the vanguard. Crassus, mounted on a superb white charger, remained motionless as the slave army advanced on a broad front. Several hundred slaves were on horseback.

Spartacus held his forces in check with his arms outspread, one hand gripping his sword.

The distance between the armies narrowed.

"Now!" shouted Spartacus.

With a great roar the slaves raced into the fray. Crassus signaled the Roman legions, which broke into a run behind the advancing Roman cavalry. Steel rang on steel as the horsemen on both sides clashed. In between and around them, gladiators and other slaves fought hand to hand with Roman foot soldiers.

Sword in hand, Spartacus fought recklessly, but with great personal courage. His eight-man bodyguard was cut down, one by one, as he battled his way toward Crassus. The mounted Roman leader awaited Spartacus's attack grimly, his own sword ready.

The last guards around Spartacus fell under a forest of Roman spears. One spear wounded the slave leader in the thigh. Limping on, he killed two centurions who flung themselves at him simultaneously. Charging at Crassus, he was stopped only a few yards from his goal by the general's bodyguards. Crassus watched impassively as Spartacus was stabbed and slashed a dozen times.

The spirit seemed to go out of the slaves with the death of their leader. Crassus's centurions quickly triumphed. Most of the rebels were killed and the rest captured. One force of slaves was killed while trying to escape from the battlefield when it ran into the arriving centurions of Pompey. Wiping out the slaves to the last man, Pompey lost no time in claiming credit for ending the Slave War.

On Crassus's orders, over 6,000 crosses were erected along the Appian Way from Capua to Rome. On each cross a captured slave was crucified. The miles of nailed victims dying a lingering death served as a terrible warning to other slaves who might be tempted to revolt.

The name of Spartacus and the memory of the two-year Slave War continued to disturb many slaveholders of the Roman republic. They had feared that their whole world had been about to turn upside down—slaves becoming masters, masters slaves.

The slave revolt caused leading Roman thinkers of the day to advocate reforms. The Stoic philosopher Posidonius, who strongly influenced Pompey, Cicero, and other leading Romans, warned that the ill usage of slaves by individual masters posed a danger to the whole community.

Concessions began to be made to slaves. As an admission that they had souls, slaves were allowed to take part in religious activities. They were permitted to join clubs for mutual help. Cicero preached that masters must be kind, considerate, and even affectionate to slaves.

The popular Roman moralist Seneca wrote his friend Lucilius, "I'm glad to learn . . . that you live on friendly terms with your slaves. That squares with your sensible outlook no less than with your philosophy. 'They're slaves.' Perhaps, but still fellow men. 'They're slaves.' But they share your roof."

He added, "Please reflect that the man you call your slave was born of the same seed, has the same good sky above him, breathes as you do, lives as you do, dies as you do! . . . Treat your slave with kindness, with courtesy too; let him share your conversations, your deliberations, and your company."

The gradual spread of more humane ideas among the upper classes continued through the Roman Empire. About fifty years later, Augustus passed decrees forbidding the mistreatment of slaves. In another fifty years, Claudius I forbade any master to kill or discard sick slaves arbitrarily. A century later, the emperor Hadrian prohibited the indiscriminate torture of slaves for evidence, and the killing of slaves by masters. The next emperor, Antoninus Pius, ordered punishment for anyone who killed or mistreated slaves, and decreed that masters who were proved to be cruel to slaves would be required to sell them.

The revolt of Spartacus and his fellow slaves had failed, but their courageous struggle eventually bore fruit for the generations who came after them.

The Slave War represented an important milestone on the way to the Emancipation Proclamation.

2

NO MORE, KING JOHN!

The Fight
for the Magna Carta

When Richard the Lion-Hearted died in 1199, his widely hated brother, John, seized the throne, sweeping aside the legitimate successor, Richard's teen-age nephew Arthur. Arthur fled to France where, with the support of French King Philip II, he challenged John's usurpation of the British crown.

John ordered Arthur and his followers kidnapped.

Several months later Arthur and twenty-two knights of his retinue were seized and chained in dungeons. Arthur was assassinated and the knights were starved to death.

These deeds angered the British people, who had enjoyed just rule under the popular Richard. There was also widespread indignation over the excesses of John's mercenary troops, who were allowed to terrorize and plunder the countryside.

The 236 barons under whose protection the towns and people lay could not stop such abuses, but the barons enjoyed a measure of revenge when King John appealed to them for troops to help in his war against King Philip, who was driving British occupation forces out of northern France.

The barons refused to send him so much as a platoon and John's army was chased out of Normandy and Anjou, which reverted to French territory.

In 1206 King John also alienated the Church by refusing to accept the pope's choice, Stephen Langton, as archbishop of Canterbury. The pope struck back by excommunicating John, relieving his subjects of their allegiance to the king. The king was enraged at the pope's denial of his right to govern. Seizing all church property in England, he outlawed the clergy. Religious Britons were terrified, seeing John's actions as the work of a madman provoking God's wrath.

Many bishops fled England. With the churches closed, anguished Britons were denied the Christian rites of baptism, marriage and burial.

To punish the barons for their opposition to his campaign in France, John ordered a study made of their individual wealth, then levied ruinous taxes on them. Barons and commoners alike complained that they received no benefits from the heavy taxes gouged by John's collectors.

Many barons also hated the king for his outrageous personal mistreatment of their families. When John traveled through the country, he stayed at the barons' castles. Often he compelled their wives and daughters to sleep with him. He once excused the wife of Sir Hugh de Neville after the latter offered the king a large sum not to molest her.

Such impropriety, perhaps more than any of his other acts, earned John the enmity of the nobility.

Some barons, deciding they had endured enough, went into open rebellion. The first to raise arms against John was William de Braose. The king ordered his wife and son kidnapped. Chained in a dungeon, they starved to death. Other revolts were ruthlessly suppressed and punished.

The pope asked the French to invade England and drive

John from the throne. Agreeing, King Philip intrigued with some English barons who promised to aid his invasion.

Informed of the barons' treachery by his spies John ordered twenty-eight young men, sons of the barons, seized as hostages. Soon afterward all twenty-eight children were hanged.

As a French armada headed for England, John panicked. Hastily making his peace with Rome, he submitted himself to the pope's authority. He agreed to restore and compensate the clergy in exile, and also to accept Stephen Langton as archbishop of Canterbury. The pope then removed John's excommunication, and the churches of England reopened.

If many British were relieved, many others were outraged by what they considered John's surrender of British power to Rome. A well-known prophet, the hermit Peter of Yorkshire, predicted that John would not be king on next Ascension Day. Furious, John had Peter and his son flung into prison. When he still held his crown on Ascension Day, he lost all fear of Peter's powers of prophecy. The hermit and his son were taken from jail, tied to the rears of horses, and dragged through the streets to a gallows, where they were hanged.

Despite John's restoration to the pope's graces, King Philip refused to recall his ships to France. They were intercepted by the British fleet off the Belgian coast and defeated in battle. John then demanded that his barons supply him with armies to invade a weakened France and retake Normandy and Anjou. Again they refused.

Furious, John sent his mercenary army to punish the barons. But he was forced to recall his men when Archbishop Langton threatened to excommunicate John again if he plunged England into a chaotic civil war against the barons.

Frustrated, John sought the armies he needed in an alliance with Germany and the Netherlands. But their joint invasion of France ended in humiliating defeat. John and his troops were forced to retreat hastily to England.

News of the king's reverses inspired Archbishop Langton to strike a blow for freedom. Summoning the leading barons, Langton showed them an old charter he had discovered in the British archives. Issued by King Henry I upon his accession to the throne, it had promised that the Crown would respect rights and liberties previously granted to the people.

"Why not," Langton asked Robert Fitzwalter, spokesman for the barons, "demand your long-lost rights now?"

Reading over the charter, the barons decided to draw up a new one and compel John to sign it upon his return to England. As a defeated monarch, he would be in poor position to resist their pressure. Langton helped them write the new charter, which opened with a statement of general principle that the king could not seize any man without justice, nor could he sell justice, nor commit an injustice.

When John returned to London, Fitzwalter and other leading barons, accompanied by a large body of armed followers for safety, met with him to present their demand. The dismayed king asked for time to consider his answer.

When the barons had left, John showed the charter to his retinue. "Why," he fumed, "amongst these unjust demands, did not the barons ask for my kingdom also? Their demands are vain and visionary, unsupported by any plea of reason whatever!"

He began putting his castles in a state of defense and increasing his mercenary army. Hearing of this mobilization, Fitzwalter knew that the king had given his answer. He summoned the barons and their troops to an armed rising.

A banner proclaimed Fitzwalter "marshal of the Army of God and Holy Church." With the blessings of Archibishop Langton, the barons marched on London.

The city's gates were thrown open by the mayor and citizens who backed the barons' cause as their own. This bloodless victory placed in rebel hands all the resources and defenses of the greatest city in the realm. The barons urged all freeholders to "abandon a king who has perjured and warred against his barons, and together with them to stand firm and fight against the king for their rights and for peace."

John fled to Windsor Castle with his supporters and the leaders of his mercenary troops. A discredited monarch, he was forced to recognize that Fitzwalter and the barons represented the popular cause. In a last desperate effort to cling to his sovereign power, he appealed to the pope to arbitrate the dispute, but the pope refused.

Abandoned on all sides, John glumly sent word from Windsor that he was prepared to meet with the barons. The jubilant rebels stipulated the time and place—near Runnymede, on June 15, 1215. Here the king was forced to sign the agreement that became famous as Magna Carta, or the Great Charter.

The charter was designed primarily to protect the human rights of the barons and their families. But it also extended these liberties "to all freeman of our kingdom, for us and all our heirs forever." The power of the king to abuse his subjects was sharply curtailed.

The king's officials could no longer steal the inheritances of heirs and widows. They could not seize the lands of debtors. Freeholders could not be forced to fight for the king overseas. The king's officials could not infringe "all the ancient liberties and free customs" of merchants in the cities and ports. Nor could he seize farms or hunting grounds to be his private sporting preserves.

New standards of justice were proclaimed. Standard penalties were imposed for felonies, making them commensurate with the degree of the crime. Workers and peasants could not be deprived of their tools, or merchants of their goods. To provide fairer trials, reforms were made in the way courts were held.

Prosecutions were not allowed on the basis of accusations, rumors or suspicions, without the supporting evidence of credible witnesses. Perhaps the most famous clause of the charter was the one that declared, "No freeman shall be taken or imprisoned . . . except by the lawful judgment of his peers, or by the law of the land. To no one will we sell, to no one will we deny, or delay right or justice."

The original clause was intended to ensure that accused barons would receive a fair and swift trial by a jury of barons in open court. Over the years, however, it came to include the right of everyone to a speedy, fair trial before a jury of fellow citizens, under due process of law.

The charter applied only to freemen, which in those days meant landholders, or freeholders, who were entitled to vote. They constituted only about 10 percent of the population. Serfs and villeins (tenant farmers) were excluded. But the number of persons who came under the protection of the Magna Carta increased steadily century after century. The Magna Carta was finally accepted as the underpinning of British law.

Subsequent revisions of the charter extended the due process of law to the common man, propertied or not. Its sum and substance gave individuals the right to say or do anything they pleased, provided they did not violate the law or infringe the legal rights of others. The king and his officials could do only what they were authorized to do by some rule of common law or statute.

King John tried several times to ignore the requirements of

the Magna Carta, but without success. When he died in 1216, a popular rhyme declared: "With John's foul deeds, England's whole realm is stinking, / As is also Hell, wherein he is now sinking."

Ironically, however, John's name went down in history attached to the Magna Carta, which he was forced to sign. He was the world's first—if unwilling—champion of human rights.

The Magna Carta was ratified many times by subsequent British kings, and became the foundation of the British constitution, which established the superiority of the rights of the people, as exemplified by Parliament, over their monarch.

When the United States broke away from the British Empire, the Magna Carta was at the heart of our own Constitution and Bill of Rights.

3

"DOWN WITH TRAITORS TO THE PEOPLE!"

The Wat Tyler Rebellion

Over a century after the Magna Carta, in 1364, English authorities were alarmed by disturbing news of an itinerant priest of Kent who was traveling through the countryside preaching revolution.

Reverend John Ball, speaking to local parishioners in church cloisters after Sunday masses, preached that there should be no more serfs and lords in England, only Britons. Did not all people descend from the same common ancestors, Adam and Eve? If God had wanted a class of serfs, would he not have created separate upper and lower classes at the very beginning?

Yet the nobility wore velvets and furs, commoners rough cloth. Nobles had wines, spices, and good bread; serfs chaff and water. Nobles dwelt in fine houses while serfs lived in the fields barely sheltered from the rain and wind. Yet it was by the labor of serfs that the nobles maintained their great estates. Any serf who dared to protest was beaten or jailed. And to whom could he complain or ask for justice?

John Ball's tirades urged the peasantry to take arms

against their oppressors: the titled landlords who enslaved them; the religious institutions with great landholdings; the lawyers, judges, and jurors who perpetuated the injustices against them. Only this way could serfs win equality and enjoy the privileges of freeholders under the Magna Carta.

Twice Ball was seized and jailed. When he was freed the second time, he urged parishioners to stop paying tithes to wealthy rectors—the clergymen in charge of parishes— whom he accused of being as corrupt as other pillars of English society. Ball was excommunicated in 1366. Parishioners were forbidden to listen to the "insane ravings of the mad priest of Kent."

The unfrocked priest continued to voice the bitter, angry feelings of the common people in England. There had been great social unrest for many years, stemming from the great plague of 1348 known as the Black Death. A third of the population had been killed off. The resulting labor shortage had led to higher wages, and the migration of workers to higher paying jobs. Many members of Parliament were landlords worried about unharvested crops. They passed laws that forced workers to stay at their jobs, and fixed wages at the old, low rates, despite a cost of living that had risen by as much as 400 percent.

Laborers who defied these laws were arrested, and released only when they agreed to return to work for their old wages. The lawyers and judges who enforced these laws were widely hated. The Church also became a target of rage because much of the land on which serfs were forced to labor was owned by monasteries and convents.

Villeins, too, were restive. These tenant farmers were compelled to work three or four days a week on the land of the lord of the manor or monastery, or on roads or other public projects. They were denied hunting and fishing rights on the lord's lands. They were forced to grind their grain only at his mill, paying whatever he charged. And they had to buy their ale from him at a monopoly price.

There was widespread impatience with the king for persisting in the endless, unpopular, unsuccessful Hundred Years' War against France. Many soldiers in the expeditionary armies deserted rather than cross the English Channel to fight. And despite the onerous taxes it imposed, the Crown was unable to prevent devastating French raids on the southeastern coast of England.

The straw that broke the camel's back was a new poll tax levied early in 1381. It required poor and rich alike to pay a shilling for every household member over age fifteen. For a rich family with six such persons, the payment of six shillings was a trifle. But for a poor family with six persons, the tax meant going hungry. To make matters worse, much of the money ended up with the Crown tax collectors.

In desperation, peasants lied about the number of people in their families over age fifteen. The reported population of England dropped almost in half. The Royal Council angrily appointed commissioners to enforce collection of the withheld shillings.

Assembling all the young men and women in a village, the commissioners announced they would examine the women for virginity as a way of determining who was old enough to be taxed. Outraged parents or friends paid the tax rather than permit the village's young women to be humiliated. Villagers who refused to pay the tax were seized and thrown into prison until it was paid.

The poll tax was bitterly attacked by John Ball. He urged peasants not to pay it despite the threat of imprisonment, and blamed the tax on John of Gaunt, the Duke of Lancaster, who was the guardian uncle of the teen-aged King Richard II.

Gaunt, Ball charged, had imposed the tax to fill a royal treasury emptied by mismanagement of the Hundred Years' War against France. Ball also denounced officials who put the cruel tax into effect—the chancellor, Archbishop Simon of Sudbury, and the royal treasurer, Sir Robert Hales. He called them "traitors to the people" who should be brought down.

Once again he was arrested, and this time sentenced to life imprisonment, chained in a dungeon of the Archbishop Sudbury's castle at Maidstone. Ball predicted defiantly that he would be set free by 20,000 supporters.

The countryside fell into an uproar. In three Kent townships the people rose en masse. They defied the commissioners to jail all of them for refusing to pay. When the commissioners tried, they were almost torn to pieces and fled for their lives.

The people of Kent now went from town to town urging other villagers to rise against the Crown officials. The rebels included not only serfs and villeins but also village craftsmen and tradesmen, who hated the restrictive labor statutes as well as the poll tax.

In May and June 1381, a people's army began to form, led by veterans of the war against France. They came armed with rusty swords and armor and age-reddened bows. Others brought axes, pitchforks, scythes, and sickles. Some were armed only with staves.

Excited by their rapidly growing numbers, the rebels began seeking out and seizing tax commissioners. The terrified officials were forced to swear on the Bible never to try to enforce the poll tax. Great lords and other notables fled to London before the advance of the rebels.

Seizing the castle at Rochester, the people's army freed a number of tax prisoners who joined them. They marched to Maidstone, where they were joined by people of that village. Here a captain was chosen—a decorated, popular veteran of the French wars named Walker ("Wat") Tyler. He derived his surname from his trade—tiling houses.

Tyler led an attack on the castle of the chancellor, Archbishop Simon of Sudbury. Breaking into the prison, the rebels freed John Ball and others from their dungeons. Ball was hailed for his defiance of Crown authorities and corrupt church officials. Voices cried out for the execution of Simon, and the ordination of Ball as the new archbishop of Canterbury. Sudbury fled to London.

As soon as his manacles were removed, Ball preached a fiery sermon to the thousands of admiring rebels who had liberated him. The rebels, he said, must abolish all differences of rank, status, and property in England. And they must kill all principal lords, Crown officials, prelates, and lawyers who tried to stop them!

The rebels surged southward through Kent. Winning recruits in every village, they soon numbered 60,000. Other rebel bands in Essex and adjacent counties gave them another 40,000 allies. Communications between the two armies led to a common goal: the capture of London.

As the rebel armies marched, they seized and burned court and tax records. Tax collectors, judges, bailiffs, lawyers, and landlords involved in sentencing tax resisters to prison were hunted down and executed. Their homes went up in flames. Some victims' heads were carried on poles by the more bloodthirsty rebels.

News of the rebel armies' convergence on London panicked the city's Crown officials, especially after Wat Tyler let it be known that the rebels' target was not fourteen-year-old King Richard, but the "traitors" who were ruining the kingdom and persecuting the people. After their execution the young king would be asked to preside over a new government that would grant human rights to all.

The boy king, alarmed, hastened from Windsor Castle to London. Taking shelter in the Tower of London, he sent messengers to urge Tyler to stop the march until the king could speak to the rebels. Richard promised to make amends for the injustices the people had suffered.

Tyler offered to meet Richard in Blackheath. The king at first agreed, then changed his mind when Sudbury and Hales warned him that it would be folly to risk exposing himself to the "shoeless ruffians." Rebuffed, the rebels marched on.

When they reached London Bridge, they found the gates closed to them by order of the city's mayor, William Walworth. But masses of poor Londoners, ardent supporters of the revolt, forced the gatekeepers to throw the city open to the people's army. Walworth was threatened with death if he interfered.

Wat Tyler's army thundered into the city on June 13, 1381. The rebels were quickly joined by thousands of poor artisans, apprentices, and others with grievances against the government. For three days the rebels ran wild in the city. Lawyers and officials were murdered, their homes sacked. The Savoy Palace of the hated John of Gaunt, who had initiated the poll tax, was burned to the ground as was the residence of the treasurer, Sir Robert Hales. Jails were broken open and the freed prisoners joined the rebels' ranks.

Soon all of London except the fortified Tower lay in the hands of Wat Tyler and his followers. Armed with new swords, battle axes, bows and arrows, they surrounded the Tower. Tyler called upon the king to yield up for execution the "traitors" sheltered in the Tower—the hated chancellor, treasurer, and other unpopular Crown officials.

Guided by his advisers, the boy king appeared in a turret. If all returned peaceably to their homes, he procalimed, he would pardon all offenses. Hoots and jeers greeted his announcement. Tyler demanded that the king issue a charter liberating the serfs and villeins.

Fearful that the crowd intended to storm the Tower, the king's advisers hastily prepared a bill for the king's signature that they hoped would appease the mob. It read:

"Richard, King of England and France, gives great thanks to his good commons, for that they have so great a desire to see and maintain their king; and he grants them pardon for all manner of trespasses and misprisions and felonies done up to this hour, and wills and commands that every one should now quickly return to his own home. He wills and commands that everyone should put his grievances in writing, and have them sent to him; and he will provide, with the aid of his loyal lords and his good council, such remedy as shall be profitable both to him and to them, and to the kingdom."

When Richard put his seal to the document, it was sent down to be read to the populace by a town crier. As its tenor became clear, a roar of disapproval drowned out the words. But instead of storming the Tower, the crowds surged back toward the city. Every lawyer and Crown official who could be found was assassinated. Several more homes of the wealthy were set afire. The king watched apprehensively from the Tower.

On the morning of June 14, almost 100,000 rebels returned

to the Tower. Tyler shouted that unless the king came out
and spoke with them, they would take the Tower by force
and slay all within. The king sent word that he would meet
with the rebels on the plain of Mile End, a summer resort
outside the city. There he would listen to and remedy grievances.

That afternoon, accompanied by many nobles, Richard
rode to the rendezvous. He was greeted by Wat Tyler at the
head of the huge rebel army. Tyler asked once more that the
king turn over all "traitors to the King and the law" to the
people for punishment. Richard replied warily that the
rebels were free to seize all alleged traitors and turn them
over to the Crown for trial.

Tyler demanded that henceforth no one could be made a
serf or villein, and that no peasant could be charged more
than four pence a year rental per acre. Furthermore, no
laborer was to be forced to work, and must be free to bar-
gain over his wages. Monopolies must be abolished, with
commoners free to buy and sell as they pleased. And the
king must agree to an amnesty for all insurgents.

Richard announced his agreement to all these terms.

"Withdraw you home into your own houses and into such
villages as you came from," he told the rebels, "and leave
behind you of every village two or three, and I shall cause
writings to be made and seal them with my seal, the which
they shall have with them, containing everything that you
demand."

The vast majority of rebels, satisfied with the king's assurances, turned homeward. Some 40,000 stayed on in London
under the leadership of Wat Tyler, acting on the king's
authority to arrest the lords they called traitors.

Returning to London, some of the rebels stormed the

Tower and captured the chancellor, Archbishop Sudbury, and the treasurer, Sir Robert Hales, among others. The sight of the hated chancellor and treasurer drove the crowd into a frenzy. Angry voices cried out against turning them over to the king for trial. Could Richard really be trusted to punish his highest officials for crimes against the people?

Tyler agreed. The prisoners were taken to Tower Hill and swiftly beheaded, along with chief tax collector John Legge and several other notables of the realm. The heads of the victims were paraded through London on poles, then raised high on London Bridge. Sudbury's archbishop's crown, nailed fast to his brow, identified him quickly to all.

Their blood lust stirred now, the rebels ran riot through the streets. Breaking into and looting homes, they seized and beheaded another 160 persons, including lawyers, Crown officials, noblemen allied to John of Gaunt, and Flemish merchants suspected of treasonous connection with the French enemy.

The following morning a mob of rebels led by freed prisoners broke into Westminster Abbey. They seized John Imworth, a prison warden noted for pitiless torture, who was dragged off and beheaded as the crowd cheered.

Wat Tyler now demanded a new meeting with the king. Further grievances had to be resolved, he said, before he would give the signal for the dispersal of the remaining Kent and Essex rebels. The king sent criers out to announce that he would meet with Tyler and his army the following day outside the city at Smithfield.

On the morning of June 15, 40,000 rebels were arrayed in a field at the designated point of assignation when the king and his retinue rode up from London. The dramatic events of that day are disputed by historians, who have written about them over the centuries. Even original sources are questionable because they were colored by the narrators' prejudices.

In the most probable version, Wat Tyler rode forward to talk to the king. Dismounting, he half-kneeled to Richard, then shook his hand roughly.

"Brother, be of good comfort and joyful," he declared, "for you shall have, in the fortnight that is to come, 40,000 more commons than you have at present, and we shall be good companions."

"Why will you not go back to your own country?" the king demanded.

"By God, we will not leave until we have a charter that includes every one of our new demands. All the lords of the realm will rue it if these demands are not met."

Tyler outlined them. There must be no more illegal procedures of law enforcement. All titles must be abolished, save that of the king. The possessions of the Church, including land and buildings, above what was needed for the sustenance of the clergy, must be divided among parishioners.

King Richard II offered to agree in substance to all these demands in a written, sealed charter, if Tyler would agree to lead his followers home promptly.

The day being fiercely hot, Tyler sent for a jug of water. Rinsing his mouth, he spat out the water near the king's feet. Then he took a jug of ale, drank it in one draught, and remounted his horse.

Outraged by Tyler's insolent manner, a valet of the king hotly denounced the rebel chief as "the greatest thief and robber in all Kent!"

Pointing his finger at the valet, Tyler demanded that he step forward away from the king's retinue. When the valet did so defiantly, Tyler ordered one of his rebel aides to dismount and behead him. Drawing a sword, the valet vowed to kill anyone who attempted to take his life. Tyler then drew a dagger and, from horseback, tried to strike the valet down.

The mayor pleaded with the rebel leader to desist. When Tyler refused, Walworth sought to arrest him. Tyler slashed at the mayor with his dagger, but Walworth was wearing armor. Drawing his sword, the mayor slashed Tyler in the neck and head. Another valet rushed forward during the scuffle and ran Tyler through with a sword two or three times.

Tyler galloped off, dying. Crying out to the rebels to avenge him, he fell from the saddle.

The enraged rebels fixed arrows to their bows and prepared to fire a volley at the king's party. Richard, spurring his horse, galloped forward and flung up his arm.

"Sirs, will you shoot your King?" he cried. "I shall now be your leader and your chief, and those of you who are loyal to me should go immediately into St. John's Field. You shall have from me all that you seek!"

By this ploy, the life of the mayor was spared. Walworth rode off to London to raise an army in defense of the king, only to find that most noblemen had fled the city in fright. He managed to assemble those who remained, along with a considerable number of armed upper-class citizens. The mayor's army then galloped to Smithfield to rescue the king.

Pouring into St. John's Field, they surrounded the rebels on all sides. The leaderless rebels were overcome with confusion. Throwing down their arms, they surrendered. Many sank to their knees to beseech the king's mercy.

Heeding his advisers, Richard granted them a pardon on condition that they leave promptly for their homes. He also presented them with a written and sealed charter acceding to their demands. His advisers whispered that he could withdraw the charter after the rebellious countryside had quieted down and been placed under armed control.

After the rebel army dispersed, the king declared martial law. His forces fanned throughout the countryside to restore order. One hundred ten persons who had committed acts of violence or defiance were seized and executed. Among them was the fiery preacher John Ball, who was taken prisoner at Coventry. The king personally attended his hanging on July 15, 1381.

Richard and the English Parliament then annulled the charter he had given the rebels.

The Peasants' Revolt of 1381 failed to end serfdom and villeinage. These systems gradually disappeared, however, as the landowners of England found that an agricultural force of rent-paying tenant farmers was far more efficient as well as less troublesome.

The Wat Tyler rebellion caused bitter debate in the British Parliament. At a meeting in November 1381, members bluntly blamed the rising on the misdeeds of royal officials. They voted to immediately abandon the hateful poll tax, and refused to consider measures of persecution against the rebels. Members warned that if a good and proper remedy for the peasants' grievances was not provided, the revolt would flare anew.

In December Parliament demanded the removal of all known "evil officers and counsellors and putting better and more virtuous . . . ones in their place." Parliament also asked the king to grant the rebels a blanket amnesty. Richard pardoned all except a few bloodthirsty leaders who had escaped capture.

Over 400 years later, when Thomas Paine wrote his famous pamphlet *The Rights of Man*, he sang the praises of

Wat Tyler. "That his memory should be traduced by Court sycophants and all those who live on the spoil[s] of a public is not to be wondered at," Paine declared. "He was, however, the means of checking the rage and injustice of taxation in his time, and the Nation owed much to his valor."

Friedrich Engels, who wrote *The Peasant War In Germany* in 1850, viewed the Peasants' Revolt in England as the earliest feudal challenge to a society based on class distinctions by those at the bottom of the ladder.

Although the revolt did not achieve most of its aims, it aroused the discontented poor of England. It was followed by risings in 1382, 1390, and 1450. The struggle of the English masses for human rights persisted through the centuries and gradually led to the establishment of a system of British justice which was extolled throughout the world as a model for other nations.

4

BREAKING THE SHACKLES

Simon Bolivar's
War of Liberation

The twenty-two-year-old Creole military student from Venezuela was exhilarated by his visit to Rome's Monte Sacro. He
stared at the mountain where the common people of Rome
had once assembled in 494 B.C. to fight injustices inflicted
upon them by the patrician Senate of the new Roman republic. Seeing the scene vividly in his mind's eye, the youth felt
a powerful sense of kinship with the early Roman plebs.
They reminded him of the poor people of his own country
suffering under Spanish rule.

Venezuelan peasants were enslaved by powerful Spanish
landlords, many of whom were members of the clergy. Corruption was widespread among Spanish officials and priests,
who controlled the government and the courts. Under Spanish law all subjects had only the legal status of "children of
the church," and were obliged to obey all religious ordi-
nances under penalty of a public whipping. Their crops and
livestock were confiscated to pay heavy taxes, and the peasants were required to sell anything the military or friars
wanted at the price offered. They were also forced into back-

breaking labor to build forts, military buildings, missions, and cathedrals in the tropical heat.

The young Simon Bolivar, remembering these injustices as he stood at the base of the Monte Sacro, knelt and vowed, "I swear by the God of my forefathers, I swear by my native land, that I shall never allow my hands to be idle, nor my soul to rest, until I have broken the shackles which bind us to Spain!"

He never forgot his oath.

From the 1520s, the Spanish ruled all of South America except Brazil for almost 300 years. Its colonies were forbidden to trade with any country except Spain. Foreign vessels were banned from South American ports. Secret agents were everywhere. Anyone caught seeking to evade the Spanish trade laws was put to death.

To keep the native population ignorant and therefore more easily controlled, most books were banned. "We do not consider education advisable in America," said one king of Spain.

Spaniards on the South American continent were divided into two classes. The Peninsulares were officials and army officers born in Spain. The Creoles were pure-blooded Spaniards born in South America. They became merchants, landowners, and intellectuals, but were treated as inferiors by the Peninsulares, who generally ignored them when making government appointments.

The relationship between the two classes was similar to that of the English-born ruling class in prerevolutionary America and American-born citizens. Many Creoles became secret revolutionaries, impatient to overturn the ruthless and backward rule of the Spanish, and set up their own governments.

Creoles felt a strong bond of sympathy for the *mestizo* class—Indians and half-castes who were slaves on the land, living in poverty.

Simon Bolivar, son of a prominent Creole, was born into this caste system at Caracas, Venezuela, on July 24, 1783. As a youth he was tutored by Simon Rodrigeuz, an intellectual who strongly admired the movers and shakers of the American Revolution. Rodriguez filled young Bolivar with reverence for such men as George Washington and Thomas Jefferson. The boy was shocked and grieved when his tutor was later arrested for conspiracy to promote revolution against Spain.

Bolivar's commitment to human rights was deepened by reading Rousseau, Montesquieu, and Voltaire. He believed firmly in the equality of all people born in the Americas.

In 1797 he was commissioned an ensign in the Spanish militia. For two years he engaged in military studies, secretly determined to use this knowledge to help liberate his countrymen.

He later traveled to Europe, where he continued his studies in Spain. He visited France, where Napoleon was being hailed as a hero for saving the French republic. The enthusiasm of the French made young Bolivar more determined than ever that some day his people, too, would live in their own republic.

On his way home Bolivar paid a visit to the United States. Talking to Americans in 1806, Bolivar greatly admired the openness and freedom he found everywhere. He was filled with enthusiasm for the new republic under Thomas Jefferson.

Exciting news reached him from Caracas. General Francisco de Miranda had led 500 men in a revolt against the

Spanish government of Venezuela. Bolivar hurried home to join the fight, but it had already been crushed by the time his ship landed.

In 1810 Bolivar joined a Creole revolt that this time succeeded in overthrowing Spanish rule. Made a lieutenant colonel in the infantry militia of the new independent Venezuela, Bolivar organized the Patriotic Society, its mission to extend the Venezuelan revolution to all of South America.

"Let us lay the cornerstone of South American liberty without fear," he urged Venezuelans. "To hesitate is to be lost!"

Spanish loyalists in Venezuela staged a counterrevolution. In a military clash against the Peninsulares in Valencia, General Miranda, now leader of the Creole army, blundered in the attack. Defeat seemed inevitable. Riding at the head of the rear guard, Bolivar flourished his sword and cried, "Long live Liberty! Follow me!" Wheeling his horse, he led the charge and the city fell to him.

The influential Spanish clergy, made up of Peninsulares, sought to turn the uneducated masses against the republican government of the United States of Venezuela. The opportunity came on the afternoon of March 26, 1812, when a terrible earthquake devastated the principal cities, leaving them in ruins. The disaster, priests told their flocks, was God's punishment for the revolution.

Bolivar worked day and night rescuing victims of the catastrophe. His efforts were ignored by the priests, who kept urging Venezuelans to repent of supporting the revolution. Many army regiments went over to the side of "Holy Spain." Wholesale defections soon left only the city of Caracas in the hands of the republicans.

In 1812 Spanish forces staged shattering victories against

the shrunken republican army. Miranda surrendered in July when Spanish authorities promised amnesty for his troops.

This marked the end of the short-lived United States of Venezuela.

Despite the pledge to Miranda, many Creoles who had fought against the Spanish were lined up against walls and shot, or sent to dungeons in chains. Bolivar's estates were seized, but he fled to the then British isle of Curaçao.

By this time, however, all South America was in revolutionary ferment. In November 1812 Bolivar made his way to New Granada, as Colombia was then known, where three rival factions were seeking to lead a revolution. Persuading them to unite in the Granadine Union, he was appointed a full colonel in the militia and given a small volunteer force.

"Let us hasten to break the chains of those victims who groan in their dungeons, awaiting salvation at your hands!" he urged New Granadians. "Do not turn a deaf ear to the lamentations of your brothers! Let us fly quickly to avenge the dead; to give new life to the dying, freedom to the oppressed, and liberty to all!"

Bolivar succeeded in driving the Spanish out of northern New Granada. Then, in spring 1813, he invaded his homeland, where he proclaimed "war to the death" against the Spanish. By August he had fought his way into Valencia and was greeted by enthusiastic crowds. Even before he marched on the capital, Caracas, a general uprising there forced the captain general and 6,000 royalists to flee.

Entering the city on August 6, Bolivar was showered with flowers and hailed by republican banners hung from balconies, proclaiming him "the Liberator of Venezuela and New Granada." On August 11, 1813, he issued a manifesto to Venezuelans:

"Nothing shall make me forget my first and only aims: your liberty and glory," he declared. "An assembly of outstanding, upright and wise men should be formally convoked to discuss and authorize the form of the government and the officials who are to run it."

Bolivar's popularity was so great that contributions for the new Republic of Venezuela poured in from peasants and patricians alike. The new government introduced liberal reforms including jury trials, freedom of speech and press, and the abolition of slavery. It looked favorably upon Bolivar's proposal that Venezuela and New Granada should unite into one strong republic, better able to resist Spanish attempts at reconquest.

When the Spanish landed reinforcements from the Iberian Peninsula, Bolivar beat them off and was awarded the title of "the Liberator" by the Venezuelan Assembly. To share this distinction with his soldiers, he founded the Order of Liberators.

King Ferdinand VII of Spain now realized that Bolivar meant to export his revolution until all South America had been liberated. Deciding that the Liberator had to be crushed, the Spanish dispatched more ships loaded with troops and enlisted an auxiliary cavalry of outlaw-cowboy mercenaries.

These *llaneros* were recruited for the Spanish by Jose Tomas Boves, a defector from Bolivar's forces. Boves was an adventurer who fought for plunder. The Spanish used him to inspire terror in the populace. In one town Boves massacred a church full of people at prayer.

Boves and his *llaneros* joined the Spanish in surrounding Caracas and threatening to destroy the republic. Bolivar led a difficult fight against them and finally inflicted losses heavy enough to force the attackers to retreat.

Boves took his revenge by destroying towns along his line of march. Men whose infirmities prevented Boves from conscripting them were put to death. Any woman or child who protested such cruelty was instantly killed.

In September 1814 Boves and the Spanish returned to Caracas in overwhelming numbers and this time Bolivar was forced to withdraw. He led thousands of citizens in an exodus from the city, rather than leave them behind to be enslaved or murdered by the enemy.

They followed Bolivar through the dense jungle in pouring equatorial rains. Many died of fever and exhaustion. Some women went mad and flung their children into ravines, jumping in after them. After a march of twenty days and nights, the exhausted survivors reached the Venezuelan city of Barcelona.

Here Bolivar managed to raise a fresh force of 3,500 men to fight Boves, but the outlaw *llaneros* scattered them in battle. Boves continued to spread terror by murdering men, women, and children in the towns and cities he seized.

Bolivar, defeated, with his army shattered, became a refugee on the English island of Jamaica. In a September 1815 article, he wrote that independence was difficult to hold even when it had been won because South Americans were not prepared for it.

"We were in the position of slaves," he explained, "not so much because of mistreatment as because of ignorance. We had no part in our own affairs, no knowledge of the science of government or administration. We were, in truth, slaves suddenly risen, without knowledge or experience."

But he predicted that one day there might be a union of all the republics of America for mutual defense and trade. To speed that day he advocated building a canal across Central America to join the Atlantic and Pacific.

Although Bolivar was defeated and alone, the Spanish still feared his influence. His own servant attempted to assassinate him, confessing that he had been bribed to do it by some Spaniards.

In 1816 Bolivar went to Port-au-Prince to persuade the president of Haiti to help mount a new expedition to free Venezuela. Winning this support, Bolivar gathered the nucleus of an army of liberation—250 refugees from New Granada. Carrying enough arms for 4,000 troops, they set sail on a fleet of seven schooners.

Off the coast of Venezuela four Spanish war vessels raced to attack them. Bolivar's fleet beat them off and captured two. He landed on the island of Margarita and was welcomed by local authorities as "Supreme Chief of the Republic."

Swiftly organizing an invasion of the mainland, Bolivar issued a stirring proclamation. "That unhappy segment of our brothers which has groaned under the miseries of slavery is now free," he declared. "Nature, justice, and policy demand the emancipation of the slaves. Henceforth there shall be in Venezuela only one class of men: All will be citizens!"

Many slaves of Venezuela, overjoyed, rushed to join Bolivar's army. Slave-owners cursed him as a traitor to his class. Other recruits were Creoles outraged by the barbarous rule of Spain's Captain General, Salvador de Moxo, whose reign of terror had taken the life of at least one member of almost every non-Peninsulare family.

In 1817 Bolivar's liberation army captured part of Venezuela. Placing this region under a civil government with independent courts, he took the field again and fought a dozen pitched battles with the Spanish. Both sides suffered heavy losses. Like Washington, Bolivar shared his troops' hardships. Suffering hunger and thirst, he slept with his men on the bare ground.

In every part of Venezuela that he liberated, Bolivar established democracy. Elections were held in all free parishes, as well as in army divisions. Elected representatives met at a special congress in Angostura in February 1819. Here Bolivar officially relinquished his authority, handing it back to the people for whose liberty he had fought.

He proposed a constitution calling for a president, elected for life, who would share powers with a two-house parliament like England's, and an independent supreme court. Bolivar asked for guarantees of trial by jury, liberty of the press, freedom of speech, and the abolition of slavery.

The congress insisted that he must accept the presidency, with a vice-president acting for him while he was off fighting the Spanish.

By May much more of Venezuela was again in republican hands. Now Bolivar led his army across the Andes into New Granada, determined to free his neighbors from Spanish tyranny, as well. For days he and his troops climbed from mountain to mountain in incessant freezing rain. Some soldiers deserted, and most of the army's horses perished.

But Bolivar urged his men on, marching 1,000 miles across the fearsome Andes in one of the most remarkable military feats in history. Emerging at Boyaca in August 1819, Bolivar led his exhausted troops to a great victory over the Spanish.

This triumph freed New Granada and secured the independence of Venezuela. Huge throngs turned out to cheer the Liberator as he led his troops into Bogota. The people celebrated with the ringing of bells, artillery salvos, skyrockets, and bonfires.

Addressing a New Granadian congress, Bolivar urged that the two countries unite as one new nation. On December 17, 1819, the congress ratified the establishment of the Republic of Colombia, which encompassed New Granada, Venezuela, and Ecuador. Ecuador was still in the hands of the Spanish, but the optimistic Colombians were confident that Bolivar would change that.

Bolivar was made the first president of the new republic, and hailed as the George Washington of South America. Taking arms again, Bolivar next liberated Panama. In June 1821, at the Battle of Carabobo, he inflicted a decisive defeat on the Spanish in Venezuela.

In 1822 he freed Ecuador, then moved south to free Peru On December 9, 1824, his forces liberated that country at the Battle of Ayacucho. The climax of his crusade, it ended Spanish rule on the continent.

Upper Peru became the Republic of Bolivia, named after Bolivar. He refused a reward of a million dollars from the new government, but was not allowed to refuse the lifetime presidency. One of his first acts in that capacity was to distribute land to the Indians.

Bolivar's revolutions created panic among the crowned heads of Europe, who feared that the uprisings would set a dangerous example in other colonies they controlled in North, South, and Central America. At a congress of monarchies in Vienna, Austrian Foreign Minister Clement von Metternich urged Europe's kings to join in a military expedition to the New World, to overthrow Bolivar's revolutionary regimes and restore the Spanish crown to Latin America.

Bolivar countered by calling the Congress of Panama in 1826. The congress worked out a Treaty of Union among eight Latin American countries. The Union, which Bolivar hoped would be strong enough to repel any European invasion, was an early version of the Organization of American States (OAS).

But nationalistic rivalry, jealousy, and suspicion undermined the treaty. Maintaining democracy was made difficult by constant clashes over shaping government policy between conservatives and liberals—further complicated by controversy over the privileges of the church. Dissension in the Republic of Colombia, which Bolivar had headed for fourteen years, eventually drove Venezuela and Ecuador to secede. Bolivar was bitterly disillusioned by the inability of individual South American nationalities to compromise their differences in the interest of continental unity and combined power.

His revolutions had brought independence to the countries of South America, but not real freedom to their people. The Spanish Peninsulares were replaced in power by aristocratic Creole civilians. They were unable to rule effectively, however, because they had no real popular support. Power remained in the hands of the military, which refused to yield it to civilian authority after fifteen years of fighting the Peninsulares.

Bolivar and the other military men who had fought for human rights in South America paid lip service to popular sovereignty. But they were basically authoritarians who kept control of the countries they liberated. They were unwilling to trust either the Creole aristocracy or the uneducated, priest-ridden masses. Independence still left the *mestizos* and mulattoes hewing wood and drawing water in poverty, even though Bolivar had freed them from slavery under the Spanish.

In January 1827 Bolivar was reelected president of Colombia. But now there was growing suspicion among liberals that he intended to annex Peru and Bolivia, rendering himself perpetual dictator of this confederacy. Distressed by their distrust, Bolivar resigned and retired to private life to prove that he had no such ambitions. In June 1828 the Colombian Congress pleaded with him to return to office. He alone, the congressmen insisted, could prevent disunity from destroying the country.

Bolivar reluctantly returned, declaring, "Allow me, then, to serve you as a simple soldier and true republican, as a citizen bearing arms in defense of the beautiful trophies of our victories: YOUR RIGHTS."

But he soon grew exasperated with the South American incapacity to make representative government work. Explaining why the Union of Colombia split up, he observed that Venezuela would always be a "military barracks," Colombia would always overflow with intellectuals, and Ecuador would always be a "convent." By this he meant that the military-minded Venezuelans, the Colombians concerned with social progress, and the church-dominated Ecuadorians could not see eye to eye.

In September 1828 over a hundred of Bolivar's opponents —those who suspected him of dictatorial ambitions—attacked the palace at Bogota, seeking to assassinate him and stir up rebellion. He escaped, and the insurrection was quickly put down by the government. But soon afterward, ill and discouraged, he resigned again and retired to private life.

Bolivar died on December 17, 1830. He died a poor man, having spent almost all of his private wealth in liberating and supporting Venezuela, Colombia, Ecuador, Peru, Bolivia, and Panama.

Bolivar's contribution to the struggle for human rights in South America was increasingly recognized after his death. He had created democratic governments in the nations he freed from the Spanish. He had sought to purify the administration of justice and protect civil liberties. And he had struggled ceaselessly to preserve freedom by seeking to create a United States of South America.

The tragedy of Bolivar was that his battles for freedom achieved no permanent goals, but had to be refought over the decades that followed. Venezuela, after Bolivar's death, has had no fewer than twenty-six different constitutions and over 100 changes of government. From 1830 to 1900 there were over fifty revolts. Of the first thirty presidents, twenty-two were generals. In the present century Venezuela cannot claim to have had more than three honest elections.

Even today constitutions of most South American republics remain nothing but blueprints for democracies. In practice they are what Bolivar gloomily called "paper and ink." In most cases the armed forces occupy their own countries like a foreign army, suppressing human rights rather than protecting them.

Occasionally, progressive forces with the support of the people break through to defeat the military oligarchies. That happened with the election of the Allende regime in Chile in 1970. Most Chileans rejoiced, believing that human rights had been secured at last. But a military junta, with the support of the Nixon administration in Washington, overthrew the government in 1973, murdering Allende and arresting and torturing political prisoners on a mass scale.

Bolivar won the first battles for human rights in South America. But those battles will have to be fought and refought in the years ahead, until civilian governments are finally able to wrest power out of the hands of the military-supported dictators. There are encouraging signs that this is beginning to happen, as in the 1979 revolution of the Sandinists of Nicaragua against the tyrannical rule of Anastasio Somoza.

5

"WE DON'T LIKE YOUNG PEOPLE TO THINK"

Mazzini's Fight for Italian Independence

Giuseppe Mazzini, a handsome young firebrand with a highly intelligent face and dark, probing eyes, was regarded with suspicion by the authorities in Genoa, Italy, where he had been born in 1805. The police had no proof, however, that he was a secret member of the revolutionary Carbonari of Piedmont when he was sent on a spy mission for them in 1830.

Nevertheless, he was arrested. When a search of his person turned up nothing incriminating, Mazzini's father demanded to know why his son had been jailed.

"He is gifted with talent," the governor of Piedmont replied, "and is too fond of walking by himself at night absorbed in thought. We don't like young people to think unless we know the subject of their thoughts."

Guilty of thinking in secret, Giuseppe Mazzini was condemned to solitary imprisonment for six months in a little cell on top of the rock fortress of Savona, on the Riviera. During these lonely, miserable months he sustained himself by dreaming up schemes for achieving a free united Italy.

With the breakup of the ancient Roman Empire, the Italian peninsula was divided into a patchwork of small states. Each was governed by a tyrannical ruler. Attempts to create an Italian nationalist movement were ruthlessly suppressed. Nationalists were arrested, drugged, tortured, and executed.

One patriot, Count Federigo Confalonieri, spent thirteen years in a cramped, unlit dungeon, legs chained and an eight-pound iron band fastened around his waist.

Before Napoleon's downfall, the French ruler brought some degree of unity to the Italian peninsula. Later, when exiled to St. Helena, he still insisted, "Italy is one nation. The unity of manners, of language, of literature, must at some future date reunite her inhabitants under a single government."

But in the 1820s, when Giuseppe Mazzini grew up, Italy was only a "geographical expression," in the contemptuous view of Clement von Metternich, who wielded great power in Europe as foreign minister of the Austrian Hapsburg Empire.

With the exception of Victor Emmanuel I—who ruled Piedmont, Sardinia, Nice, and Savoy—the rulers of the Italian states were all foreign despots imposed upon the Italian people by Austria. Their regimes were characterized by heavy taxes, spying by secret police, censorship, and imprisonment for political opposition. Young Italians were conscripted into the Austrian army.

Discontent with these monarchies was most intense among the educated middle and upper classes, and among urban wage earners. Strongly nationalistic, many were arrested for conspiring to unite Italy under native rule. Many working-class Italians cared little whose flag flew over them. Some were resigned to Austrian control. A few of the most conservative were even pro-Austrian.

The struggle for Italian unity was part of an international republican movement sweeping Europe. It was aimed at overthrowing all tyrannical monarchies, and replacing them with constitutional governments. The republicans were fought by Metternich, who united the kings of Europe to suppress dissent and revolution. Anyone demanding a constitution was arrested for subversion.

In Italy young Mazzini wrote, "I see the people pass before my eyes in the lives of wretchedness and political subjugation, ragged and hungry, painfully gathering the crumbs that wealth insultingly tosses to it." He was confident that God would soon manifest himself to the people, who would then rise together—"brothers in one faith, one bond of equality and love"—to win republican government.

As a student of law, Mazzini read widely in the writings of democratic thinkers. "Without liberty," he wrote, "there is no true morality." He threw himself heart and soul into the Risorgimento ("renaissance") movement of secret societies in all parts of the peninsula dedicated to Italian unification.

The most important secret society was the Carbonari, or "Charcoal Burners." Organized in 1808, its members were dedicated to freeing southern Italy from French rule and obtaining constitutional liberties. Pledging to "deliver the lamb from the wolf," they operated secretly under a revolutionary flag of red, blue, and black.

The French Revolution of 1830 sent a wave of hope rippling through other republicans in Europe, who redoubled efforts to end royal tyranny in their own countries. Many, like Mazzini, were caught and flung into prison.

During his imprisonment in the fortress of Savona, Mazzini concluded that the Carbonari—after twenty-two years of failure—was suffering from an aging and unimaginative leadership. What was needed, he was convinced, was a new, dynamic organization led by young men like himself.

"Place the young at the head of the insurgent masses," Mazzini wrote. "You do not know what strength is latent in these young hands, what magic influence the voice of the young has on the crowd; you will find in them a host of apostles for the new religion."

Set free, he left for Marseilles, where he organized the Association of Young Italy. Young revolutionaries were urged to spread propaganda for nationalism and freedom not only in Italy but throughout Europe. Putting aside all personal interests, Mazzini gave every waking hour to the Risorgimento. His only income was a tiny quarterly allowance sent by his family.

Starting with nine followers, Mazzini worked day and night writing articles and letters, and printing propaganda.

"We were reduced to the extreme of poverty," he wrote later of those hectic days, "but we were always cheerful."

His leaflets and newspaper, *Young Italy*, were smuggled into Italy in bales of merchandise, sometimes even in sausages, by travelers and Italian sailors. Passed from hand to hand, they were eagerly read by Italian youth, who thrilled to Mazzini's message that a democratic republic, free of all royal and religious restraints, was the only form of government consistent with the dignity of a self-respecting people. They were inspired by his vision of a free united Italy that would help snap the royalist chains of other Europeans.

Chapters of Young Italy began spreading through north and central Italy, sworn to Mazzini's motto, "God and the people." The organization attracted students, young professionals, and young men of the mercantile classes. Within two years the new underground movement had over 50,000 members.

Mazzini had little patience with those who feared to join Young Italy because of the opposition of the church or the threat of arrest. "Italians *could* and therefore *should* struggle for liberty of country," he insisted, and added, "While we pity men who do not know the truth, we despise men who, though they know the truth, dare not speak it."

But Italian moderates felt that Mazzini was an impractical radical. They worked instead for an amelioration of the people's misery by supporting unification of Italy under a limited monarchy or under a federation of Italian states headed by the pope.

The moderates were encouraged when an Italian, Charles Albert, who had been a Carbinari conspirator ten years earlier, became king of Piedmont and Sardinia. They looked to him to drive the Austrians out of the Italian peninsula and create a federation of Italian states.

In April 1831 Mazzini published an open letter to Charles Albert, urging him to lead the impending struggle for Italian independence. All Italy, Mazzini promised, would rally to the king if he would draw his sword against Austria.

"Do this and we will gather round you," Mazzini promised, "we will give our lives for you, we will bring the little states of Italy under your flag. But if you will not, others will do it without you, or against you."

Charles Albert, who had long since forsaken liberalism, ordered that anyone who was caught reading Mazzini's newspaper would be fined and jailed for two years. Italy was plastered with posters calling for Mazzini's arrest, if he dared to cross the frontier.

But his challenge to Charles Albert was clandestinely reprinted and circulated throughout Italy. By April 1833 Young Italy had become a powerful underground organization in every part of the country. Preparations were being made for a general uprising against Austria.

Metternich's and Charles Albert's spies worked day and night to trace key figures in the conspiracy. Then police made midnight raids on hundreds of homes in Piedmont. Prisoners were tortured, tried, and executed. A dozen youths were put to death for having been caught reading publications of Young Italy, and for refusing to expose the persons from whom they obtained them.

Mazzini, still in Marseilles, was tried in absentia and sentenced to death. The uprising, scheduled to begin in Genoa, was aborted.

Mazzini left France for Geneva, where he organized German, Polish, and Italian political exiles into a guerrilla army to liberate Savoy. This new plot failed when it was exposed by one leader who proved to be a French spy.

Unsuccessful in Italy, Mazzini turned to fomenting revolution elsewhere in Europe. Political exiles in Switzerland helped him organize the Association of Young Europe in April 1834. Branches were set up in their homelands—Young Poland, Young Germany, and Young Switzerland—dedicated to "liberty, equality and fraternity for all mankind."

Mazzini's new move provoked the wrath of Metternich. At the end of 1836 Metternich's Holy Alliance of European monarchs put pressure on Switzerland. Many of Mazzini's followers were jailed, then expelled. In 1837 Mazzini left Switzerland for England, the only country in Europe where he was not subject to arrest.

From London he continued conspiring with political agitators all over Europe. His health suffered from his endless struggle with poverty. He was forced to pawn everything he owned, even his winter coat and boots, for food and rent money.

Managing to earn a few pounds as a literary critic, he became a friend of Thomas Carlyle. The essayist profoundly disagreed with Mazzini's faith in the people as the vanguard of revolution.

"The people!" Carlyle scoffed. "The ignorant, blind, vicious masses . . . to be regarded as teachers, leaders, guides? . . . No! In verity they were to be taught, led, guided, if need be constrained to obey the superior wisdom and virtue of the chosen few!"

Mazzini remained unshaken in his vision of a democratic Europe to be brought about by a rising of the masses. Nor did he allow himself to be discouraged when Metternich's forces suppressed all attempts to topple monarchy.

"The tree of liberty," Mazzini quoted Jefferson, "grows stronger when watered by the blood of martyrs."

Young Italy attracted a dynamic new leader in Giuseppe Garibaldi, a merchant sailor. He quickly rose in the movement to become its man of action, with Mazzini serving as its inspiration and chief propagandist.

In 1834 they joined forces in Italy to lead a local rising which collapsed. Garibaldi was captured and condemned to death, but escaped to South America, where he lived for twelve years as leader of guerrilla movements for independence. Mazzini returned to England to continue stirring up rebellion from what he considered a safe refuge.

Ironically, the letters Mazzini sent to Italy to provoke revolution became instruments used to prevent it. English police spies, opposed to revolutionists, opened his mail. Information on Young Italy militants was reported to Metternich, who ordered them arrested and executed. Two captured leaders went to their death singing a Risorgimento song, "Who dies for his country has lived long enough." Sympathetic soldiers of the firing squad wept and deliberately fired over their heads.

One of the doomed pair called out, "Courage, do your duty. We, too, are soldiers!" The next volley killed them. They died crying, "Long live liberty, long live the nation!"

The executions led to the revelation that Mazzini's mail had been systematically violated for over four months. The news caused an indignant uproar in England's House of Commons.

Despite such setbacks, Mazzini kept the revolutionary flame burning throughout Europe. His inspiring accounts of the daring exploits of Garibaldi in South America were eagerly read, and paved the way for Garibaldi's return to Italy as a revolutionary hero and leader after long years of exile.

In 1846 a new pope, Pius IX, gave fresh hope to Italian republicans by releasing 1,000 political prisoners from jail and announcing an amnesty for all political offenders in the Papal State.

Promising economic reforms, streetlights, railways, and other welcome changes, Pius IX gave Rome a municipal government with an advisory council of citizens. The Papal State even entered into a customs union with Tuscany and Piedmont, the first move toward Italian unity.

Delighted Italians pressed the new pope for constitutional rights. Skeptical but hopeful, Mazzini wrote the pope a conciliatory letter in 1847. He promised to put Young Italy's forces at the Vatican's disposal if the pope would agree to lead the fight to break the Austrian stranglehold on the Italian peninsula. "We shall not consider that we are paying too dear a price for the privilege," he declared, "if it be with the blood of us all."

But the pope had no intention of attacking the Catholic Austrian Empire, or of permitting constitutional government. Responding to the people's grievances as an act of mercy was one thing. Turning over control of the state to the people was something else again!

The rumblings of change in the Papal State, however, alarmed Metternich. He warned the kings of Europe that they must not yield to any popular demand for constitutional government. Kings ruled by divine right, he pointed out, and would lose their power if they agreed to share it with the people.

But change was being made inevitable by the Industrial Revolution, particularly in the advanced countries of Europe. Labor-saving machinery was throwing many out of jobs, and bad harvests had sent food prices soaring.

The masses might endure repression of their human rights out of fear of the police, but they could not tolerate starvation for themselves or their families. In 1844 factory workers rioted in Austrian-held Prague. Storming the mills and destroying the machines, the workers were shot down by royal troops.

The times grew rapidly stormier. In 1845 and 1846 European potato crop failures created peasant unrest. Food shortages angered workers in the cities. In Paris, where one out of three workers died so poor that the city had to pay for the funeral, the capitalist system itself came under attack.

"Property is theft," insisted anarchist Pierre Proudhon. Karl Marx and Friedrich Engels prepared the *Communist Manifesto*. They predicted an inevitable clash between industrial capitalism and the proletariat it had created.

In 1847 Mazzini organized the People's International League, which arranged cooperation among the various independence movements in Europe. He called for the right of all nationalities to self-determination, and for the free exchange of people, goods, ideas, and information.

"The map of Europe has to be re-made," Mazzini wrote. The continent, he warned, was sleeping on a volcano that seethed with repressed revolt against oppression. If all nationalities were not freed from alien rule, they would overthrow their rulers. "A great general war is drawing near," he predicted, "between the principles of progress and reaction, of liberty and despotism."

Events began to peak toward a climax during 1847. Liberals won upset election victories in Switzerland and Hungary. Food riots in Berlin led to the formation of a united German-Prussian Diet pledged to reforms. French anti-monarchists insisted that King Louis Philippe cancel a poll tax designed to prevent the poor from voting.

The storm broke in February 1848.

Great masses of French national guardsmen, republicans, democrats, and workers rioted in the streets of Paris. Fearing the guillotine, Louis Philippe abdicated and fled to England. Leaders of the revolt proclaimed the Second French Republic. New elections made Napoleon's nephew Louis president.

The February Revolution in France touched off the powder kegs that Mazzini and other revolutionists had been patiently filling all over Europe. The upheavals affected the lives of over 260 million people.

Mazzini rushed to Paris to assemble all Italian exiles there into the new Italian National Association, dedicated to throwing the Austrians out of Italy and creating a free government. In front of the new French Parliament, the premier told Mazzini, "Since France and Italy form but one single name in their common desire for liberal regeneration, we say to Italy that . . . if an attack were to be made on her soil . . . it would be the sword of France that would be placed at her disposal!"

Although still condemned to death in his native land, Mazzini sped to Milan to join an anti-Austrian rising that had broken out in the city. The revolt spread quickly to other cities. Austrian troops fired on unarmed citizens and students. Rebel leaders were thrown into jail on charges of high treason. Martial law was declared, permitting the execution without trial of any person two hours after arrest.

In the midst of the turmoil word came that revolution had also broken out in Vienna, the seat of Austrian tyranny. Metternich had been forced to resign and flee, and the emperor had been compelled to grant freedom of the press, and other reforms. Overjoyed, the citizenry of Milan rose *en masse* against their oppressors.

They threw up over 1,700 street barricades made of carriages, pianos, pulpits, house beams, and furniture. The Milanese behind these barricades, even though only a few hundred of them had arms, bravely fought off 15,000 Austrian troops. Women and young boys fought beside the men, hurling tiles, stones, bottles, and crockery. Housewives poured boiling water on troops from upper windows and the roofs of houses.

Rich Milanese opened their palaces to the poor whose homes had been wrecked by the Austrians. Milanese who took prisoners treated them far more generously than the Austrians, who tortured and burned to death Italian men, women, and children seized at the barricades.

When a particularly vicious Austrian official was captured

hiding in a hayloft, a Milanese mob called for his death. But Italian leader Carlo Cattaneo told them, "If you kill him, you will be acting justly. If you spare him, you will be acting nobly." The trembling prisoner was spared—a human rights gesture that indicated the kind of decent new society the Milanese were fighting for.

"Brave citizens, let us keep our city pure," urged a revolutionary Council of War proclamation. "Let us not condescend to revenge ourselves by the blood of these miserable satellites. . . . It is true that for thirty years they have been the scourge of our families and the abomination of the country, but . . . . Punish them, rather, with contempt."

The Austrian troops were driven out of Milan, which was then proclaimed the capital of a provisional republic. The jubilant Milanese gave Mazzini a torchlight victory parade. When he urged them to help drive Austrians out of the rest of Italy, they joined Venetians in freeing their city, which became a republic. The autocratic rulers of Parma and Modena were also driven out.

Many European monarchs were badly shaken by the wave of revolutions sweeping Italy and the rest of the continent. With Metternich no longer there to hold them in line, one monarch after another began granting constitutions to his people.

Mail surveillance, censorship, and political arrests were stopped. The kings hoped that these concessions to human rights would suffice, and permit them to remain on their thrones.

King Charles Albert of Piedmont now prudently decided that the time had come to heed Mazzini's urging and declare war on Austria. When Italian moderates rose against the Austrians in Lombardy and were being hurled back in fierce battles, Charles Albert became a hero by marching his troops to the insurgents' rescue.

Lombardy was freed. Now the whole Italian peninsula was in ferment. Garibaldi returned from South America to join Mazzini in leading some of the uprisings. Overjoyed Italians were convinced that liberation and unification of Italy were at hand.

But that summer the Austrians mounted a major counterattack. Charles Albert's troops were driven out of Lombardy, Venetia, Parma, and Modena. To the dismay of the Moderate Party, the king negotiated to hold Piedmont by agreeing to Austrian rule of Venice. Mazzini angrily warned Italians that their only hope of freedom now lay in trusting the people, not any king.

In early 1849 the people of Tuscany overthrew their ruler, Grand Duke Leopold II. Proclaiming a republic, they asked the people of Rome to join them. Mazzini was named to the new government. But now the pope denounced the revolution, and refused the Roman citizens' demand for democratic government.

Outraged, Mazzini cried for an uprising against the Vatican. The pope fled to the protection of the hated king of Naples, Ferdinand II, whose troops burned homes, raped and murdered women, and slaughtered children and old men.

In March 1849 Rome was declared a republic. Mazzini was elected the leading member of a triumvirate of rulers. He vowed to make Rome the symbol of the kind of government he had preached for so long—by "God and the people."

One month later French troops attacked the city. Garibaldi led a valiant resistance, but the French finally won Rome in July 1849. Vatican rule was restored, and Mazzini

left Rome. By that summer the Austrians had regained control of the peninsula. The puppet monarchs returned to the
thrones from which they had fled.

The uprising of the Italian people collapsed primarily because they failed to join together as a unified army against
their oppressors. The only constitution which endured was
that of Piedmont. There Victor Emmanuel II had succeeded
his father, Charles Albert, who abdicated after being defeated by Austria. More and more Italians now looked to
Victor Emmanuel as their last hope of a free unified Italy.

The Austrians punished all Italians who were suspected of
opposing Hapsburg rule. Men and women were whipped for
trifling offenses. One women was flogged and had her hair
pulled out for speaking disrespectfully of the Austrian governor. When fifteen Milanese men and women hissed at a
woman who displayed an Austrian flag on her balcony, they
were publicly flogged, and the women were stripped for the
beating. In Rome, Italians known to have served the republic
were sent to prison or to work aboard sea-going galleys.

A discouraged Mazzini returned to London in 1850. To
raise new funds for the cause, he organized the Society of
the Friends of Italy. In 1853 they supported his secret return
to Milan to lead a new revolution there, with a simultaneous
uprising in Bologna. The Austrians, tipped off, crushed the
rebellion. Mazzini's prestige waned.

Refusing to give up, he plotted patiently for another four
years. Then in 1857 he spurred new risings in Genoa, Leg-
horn, and Naples. These, too, failed, and Mazzini was once
more placed under sentence of death.

The constant failure of revolution disillusioned Mazzini's
countrymen. More and more they looked to Victor Emman-

uel and his troops to free them. From London Mazzini protested, "The Italian people are led astray by a delusion." Nevertheless he, too, was reduced to pleading with Victor Emmanuel to fight for Italian unification, pledging the support of republicans.

The king, who sought to expand Piedmont into a north Italian kingdom, finally ordered his army to drive the Austrians out of Italy. At a signal from Mazzini, revolts broke out in Tuscany, Modena, Parma, and Romagna.

In 1859 Garibaldi and his Red Shirts invaded Sicily. Conquering the island, Garibaldi pressed on, with Victor Emmanuel at his side, to take Naples. A tide of nationalism swept over the peninsula, carrying off all alien rulers.

On February 18, 1861, the first national parliament representing the north and south of Italy met at Turin. Amid fervent enthusiasm the united Kingdom of Italy was proclaimed on March 17, 1861. Victor Emmanuel II was declared "by the grace of God and will of the nation King of Italy."

Only Venice and Rome remained outside the new kingdom. From abroad Mazzini insisted that the king's army press on and free them, too. But Victor Emmanuel refused to alienate the Vatican. When Garibaldi organized his own attack on Rome, in 1862, the king declared him a rebel. Captured by Piedmont troops, Garibaldi was wounded, arrested, and imprisoned in Naples. Many of his followers were shot without trial.

Mazzini appealed to the Piedmont ministry to free Garibaldi. "All Italy is wounded and a prisoner with him," Mazzini protested. He worked day and night raising funds to win the freedom of the jailed Garibaldi and his men.

Finally released in 1864, Garibaldi joined Mazzini in London. At a celebrated gathering he toasted Mazzini, declaring, "He alone had kept alive the sacred fire; he alone watched while others slept . . . filled with the love of country, filled with love for the cause of country."

In 1865 the Italian people expressed their affection for the exiled Mazzini. Although he was still officially under a death sentence for treason, he was elected in absentia to the new Italian Parliament. But Mazzini declined his seat, refusing to swear an oath of allegiance to any monarch—even the one who had united Italians at last.

The following year a political settlement brought Venice into the new Italian union. In celebration, Victor Emmanuel declared a general amnesty for all political prisoners and exiles. Mazzini rejected what he called an "offer of oblivion and pardon for having loved Italy above all earthly things."

Going to Switzerland, he entered a new conspiracy with Garibaldi to liberate the Papal States and make Rome the capital of a republican Italy. In 1869, at the demand of Victor Emmanuel's government, the Swiss expelled Mazzini. When he persisted in the scheme, he was arrested at sea in 1870 and imprisoned at Gaeta for two months.

Victor Emmanuel's advisers warned him that Mazzini and Garibaldi had the support of the Italian people. If the king failed to complete the unification of Italy, his monarchy might topple. So, without crediting either patriot for his change of mind, Victor Emmanuel ordered his troops to take Rome. On September 20, 1870, after only a few hours of fighting, the people of Rome hailed them as deliverers.

Another general amnesty in 1871 freed Mazzini. He died a year later in Pisa, on March 10, 1872, worn out and disillusioned because the unification of Italy, which he had done more than anyone to inspire and bring about, had resulted in the establishment of a monarchy rather than a republic.

The Italian Parliament voted a unanimous expression of national sorrow. Its president called Mazzini a patriotic model of disinterestedness and self-denial who had dedicated his whole life to his country's freedom.

Seventy-four years later, on June 10, 1946, Italian men and women voted to end the monarchy and establish a republic, fulfilling the lifelong dream of Giuseppe Mazzini.

6

"WHO CARES WHETHER WE LIVE OR DIE?"

The Chinese General Strike of 1922

The year was 1922, the place China. A China undergoing rapid change through industrialization. Western capital had built factories of all kinds, taking advantage of cheap Chinese labor and raw materials. The factories were filled with coolies, peasants, women, young boys and girls. Many of them had been sold into jobs as virtual slaves for four or five years and were not allowed to leave the heavily guarded, high-walled premises day or night without special permission.

"I used to work at a textile factory," recalled one Chinese woman years later. "In those days I was often beaten by my superiors and was forced to work day and night. I was not even given time to eat lunch. I had three children but all died of malnutrition."

Foreign factory owners and foremen patrolled the factory floors with whips in their hands. Anyone working too slowly or falling asleep at a machine from exhaustion or hunger was lashed into accelerated activity. It was not unusual for a reluctant worker to be killed at the job as an object lesson.

His body would simply be thrown out onto the street for a

"death wagon" to pick up. In Shanghai up to 50,000 corpses a year—including Chinese who had starved to death in the street—were collected and buried in paupers' graves. Tens of thousands of workers, too worn out or too old to work as fast as they once could, were fired each year and sent back empty-handed to their native villages to die.

The working day was fourteen hours, seven days a week. The low wages barely kept a worker alive. Workers were forced to live in cramped, dark and filthy tenements. Disease was rampant.

Many small workshops were owned by Chinese. The owners bought little boys and girls from famine-ravaged regions, and worked them as slaves at primitive machines. After work the children dropped into exhausted sleep under the machines on dirty cotton quilts. Many died of fatigue and malnutrition.

Chinese workers in the Shanghai textile mills were paid only nine dollars a month, but were charged exorbitant rents for the miserable sheds in which they slept. There were absolutely no health or safety precautions on the job. Accidents were common. American-owned factories employed up to 3,000 women to make hairnets under wretched conditions. Many were little girls, although the minimum age of employment was supposed to be fourteen. Factories owned by the British and Japanese were even worse.

In foreign-owned coalfields, small naked boys were used to cut coal from mine faces. Harnessed to heavy basketloads, they dragged these up to the surface on their hands and knees. Working twelve-hour days, seven days a week, they were awarded free coffins when they died—usually at an early age.

Writer Pearl S. Buck visited foreign mills employing Chinese workers in the early 1920s. "They were so hopeless," she reported. " 'No one can help us,' they wept. 'Who wants us? No one, anywhere. Who cares whether we live or die, or has ever cared? . . . What can we do? Nothing—and we know it.' "

Mrs. Buck contrasted the desperate misery of poor workers with the wealthy life style of foreigners in China: "Nobody seemed to care about anything. Everybody was out for spending money and having a good time."

Manufacturers had no trouble getting all the workers they wanted. In addition to children sold by hungry parents, hundreds of thousands of peasants had been driven off the land during World War I. They had flocked into China's cities looking for work in the burgeoning new factories. The coolie population, which had never had enough to eat and often slept under bridges, was easily enticed to work for a bowl of rice and a roof over their heads.

Manufacturers often made a profit of 1,000 percent or more on their operations. Japanese industrialists provided workers with dormitories, which served in effect as prisons to lock in labor. With an infinite supply of cheap labor, factory owners were able to set any terms of employment they wished.

Chu Teh, later head of the Chinese Red Army, recalled Shanghai as a "hell of limitless luxury and corruption for the few, and limitless work and suffering for the masses." No country on earth, he said, had been as miserable as China following World War I.

The Chinese workers were also embittered by the contempt in which they were held by foreigners. A Chinese who did not get out of a Westerner's way on the street was imperiously shoved aside. In the Shanghai International Settlement some parks and buildings bore the insulting sign: *Chinese and Dogs Not Allowed.* In their own country the

Chinese were not only exploited but also treated as a lower species.

Journalist Vincent Sheehan noted, "Against any mention of these facts the Shanghai foreigner, sipping his cocktail reflectively in the cool recesses of one of his clubs, would reply . . . that, in any case, the Chinese were an inferior race, had never been used to anything but starvation and overwork, misery and oppression, and consequently 'don't feel anything —not, at least, as we do.' I never met anybody in Shanghai who revealed the slightest feeling of shame . . . in thus taking advantage of human misery in its most appalling forms. On the contrary, the Shanghai foreigners felt . . . horrified at the rising Chinese demand for better conditions of life and a recognized share in the spoils."

This demand was first made by 200,000 Chinese workers who had been sent to Europe during World War I to provide cheap labor for the Allies, replacing workers drafted for the trenches. In Europe they learned to read and write and many had been greatly impressed by the ideas of European workers, as well as by their higher standard of living.

The Chinese workers returned home determined to better their own conditions. They began organizing Western-style labor unions, helped by Chinese students who had gone to France as part of a work-study program. Many of these students returned as converts to socialism, communism, or anarchism.

Strikes broke out sporadically. As some unions won concessions, their ranks began to swell. Chinese seamen quickly formed their own union. From their very low wages, they were forced to pay kickbacks to foremen in order to work. (By arrangement with the shipowners, the foremen had been given the exclusive right to select the ships' crews for voyages.) Foreign seaman were paid 500 percent more than Chinese seamen.

In British-held Hong Kong, a British seamen's union won a big increase in wages. The newly formed General Industrial Federation of Chinese Seamen promptly demanded a 10 to 50 percent wage increase of their own. The union also asked for recognition, the right to supply Chinese seamen for voyages, and improved working conditions at sea.

Union leaders Su Chao-jen and Lin Wei-ming pointed out that their members had had no wage increase for eight years, while the cost of living had risen by over 200 percent. They submitted the union's demands three times to the Western shipowners, but were ignored. The shipowners had been forced to take the demands of trained British seamen seriously. But Chinese workers were as plentiful as seaweed; there was no need to placate them.

In January 1922 Su Chao-jen finally issued a call for a strike. About 1,500 Chinese deck hands and stokers responded. The strike was supported by other Hong Kong workers who responded to an appeal for Chinese patriotism and worker solidarity. Within twenty-four hours every Chinese dockworker in the great port of Hong Kong walked out. Servants in the homes of rich Europeans went on strike. The issue escalated swiftly from just the Chinese seamen's grievances to a widespread protest against the treatment of all Chinese by European overlords.

The British governor of Hong Kong declared martial law. Proclaiming the Chinese seamen's union an unlawful organization, he ordered police to shut down the union's headquarters, seize its papers, and remove its sign. A warrant was issued for the arrest of Su Chao-jen, who fled into hiding. On February 8 the dockworkers' union was also declared illegal.

Striking seamen left Hong Kong for Canton, establishing a new headquarters under the sympathetic government of Sun Yat-sen. Picket lines were set up at the port. As ships berthed, their Chinese crews were urged to join the strike. By the end of the first week 6,500 seamen were out. By the end of the month nearly 30,000 men had struck, and 151 ships were tied up in Canton. The strike began to affect not only the big shipping companies but the whole economic life of Hong Kong.

Thus isolated, Hong Kong could not produce enough commodities to meet its inhabitants' needs. The strikers' shutdown of the shipping lanes caused an acute shortage of grain and other food supplies in the colony. The price of rice soared 60 percent, meat 30 percent.

The British authorities sent ships manned by British seamen to Canton for supplies. But they were thwarted by Canton's coolies, who united in support of the seamen and refused to load the ships. Hong Kong, the proudest bastion of British power in China, was paralyzed for almost two months.

The colonial government, through Secretary for Chinese Affairs Halifax, tried desperately to bring about a settlement. Halifax was aided by rich Chinese merchants, called compradores, whose business was also severely affected by the strike. A series of negotiations took place between the seamen, on one hand, and Halifax and the shipping companies, on the other.

The two sides clashed on the size of the raise to be granted, union hall hiring rights, the reinstatement of all strikers without penalties, and the restoration of the union's legal status. Halifax offered to recognize the union if it were reorganized under another name, to save face for the Hong Kong government. As a point of honor, the seamen refused.

By this time the strike's political overtones had gone far beyond the demands of the seamen. All Chinese workers in Hong Kong saw the strike as the first major challenge of Western imperialist power by exploited and mistreated Chinese labor. They felt the first tinges of hope that if the seamen could win, their own lives might change as well. Recognizing that the key to such a victory lay in the solidarity of all Hong Kong workers, they rallied to the seamen.

The colony's transport workers declared a sympathy strike, urging workers of every kind to join them. Almost overnight a general strike paralyzed the colony further.

Waves of excitement ran through all China. Support for the strike came from workers all over the country. In Changsha Province, Mao Tse-tung helped organize a series of strikes, including a miners' strike at Anyuan. The railway workers on the Peking-Hankow railway struck and, by tying up the railroads, won their demands in just two days.

This had never happened before in China. Western powers with investments in China grew apprehensive. Dismayed by the political overtones of the strikes, they viewed them as revolutionary.

Western agents fought back by recruiting scab labor and seeking to split labor unity by bribes. Leaders of the seamen were arrested, imprisoned, beaten up, and even murdered.

The seamen firmed their ranks and thwarted every attempt to break their strike. Seamen in the ports of Swatow and Wuchow joined the strike in a gesture of solidarity. In Hong Kong women workers pooled their meager funds to keep the general strike going as long as possible.

Financial support also came from the Canton government of Sun Yat-sen, who had established a branch of his Kuomintang party among Chinese seamen on foreign ships eight years earlier. They had carried his messages appealing for support to overseas Chinese. In 1920 Sun had also sponsored the formation of the seamen's union. He now gave the strike his full backing.

Sun Yat-sen's support also made it possible for help to be given by Canton's trade associations. Canton mechanics, railwaymen, and craftsmen took Honk Kong strikers, forced to flee from British police, into their homes.

Railwaymen in various parts of the country contributed a day's pay to the strikers. Support also came from overseas. Russian workers took up collections and forwarded them to the seamen. Contributions and expressions of solidarity came from Chinese seamen in Siam, the Philippines, Yokohama, and Calcutta.

When the British tried to recruit strikebreakers in Shanghai, seamen's guilds pressured recruits to change their minds about scabbing. Two guild leaders were arrested for interfering with recruitment, but a storm of protest forced their release.

By the beginning of March the number of strikers had increased to 120,000. Their ranks now included vegetable sellers, tramway employees, basketmakers, and electricians. Chinese workers everywhere were jubilant at this display of national defiance. Let the imperialists try to operate their settlements without the Chinese workers whose human rights they had violated!

On March 3 more Hong Kong strikers sought to abandon the colony for Canton. They were stopped en route to the dock, in the suburb of Sha-t'ien, by British police who fired upon them. Instead of intimidating the Chinese, this new act of violence infuriated them into a boycott of everything and everyone British. Life in the crown colony became totally disorganized.

Five days later the harassed Hong Kong government finally surrendered. The jubilant strikers won their demands with wage increases of 15 to 30 percent and union hall hiring. All of the unions that had been outlawed were again legalized. Arrested and beaten-up strikers were released with a public apology. And the police officer who had torn down the sign at the seamen's union headquarters was required to put it back up.

Over 200,000 Chinese celebrated their victory on the streets of Hong Kong. The first Chinese defeat of foreign imperialism aroused wild enthusiasm throughout the country. The victory of the Hong Kong workers, declared Chu Teh, was the opening shot of the Chinese masses in their struggle for the liberation of their nation.

The seamen's strike had repercussions in London. Winston Churchill rose in the House of Commons to defend the governor of Hong Kong for having resisted the strikers' demands. He was howled down by Labor MPs, who pointed out that the governor's actions had led to a fifty-day paralysis of Britain's most important port in the Orient, and had also infuriated the entire Chinese population against the British Empire.

The success of the strike, which now threatened all foreign settlements with further Chinese challenges, led to the call for a National Labor Congress in Canton on May 1, 1922. This meeting was attended by 162 Chinese delegates representing 12 cities, over 100 trade unions, and 300,000 union members. Among them were prominent members of the Kuomintang and the Communist party, both of which were to play crucial roles in the anti-imperialist fight for Chinese sovereignty.

The labor congress declared its intention to unionize

workers throughout China. It demanded an eight-hour work-day, civil rights and educational opportunities for workers, and the end of whipping and other cruel treatment of factory help. The congress adopted two Communist slogans: "Down with Imperialism!" and "Down with the Warlords!" The warlords were local Chinese dictators who ruled their provinces through private armies.

The congress was the first meeting in which labor organizations from various parts of the country had official contact with each other. These groups agreed to work together toward common goals.

The seamen's victory and the National Labor Congress precipitated a new tidal wave of strikes all over China during 1922 and early 1923. Workers rebelled against being whipped for slowing down at the end of a fourteen-hour workday, and against being paid starvation wages while living costs soared.

Alarmed Westerners and Chinese warlords tried to suppress the strikes with troops and police. But in Kiangsi Province, warlord troops that were sent against striking coal miners refused to open fire on the workers. The authorities attempted to arrest the strike leader, but he was surrounded by thousands of strikers who fought off every attempt to seize him.

Refusing to be intimidated by violence, the newly militant workers of China won most of the strikes they called. They demanded that the national government at Peking adopt a new charter of labor rights, and they pressured newspapers all over China to report their demands.

The Peking government, controlled by rich warlords, refused to heed the workers. But authorities in Kwangtung Province repealed a Peking law that made strikes illegal. The proposed charter of labor's rights impressed Chinese workers and became their agenda for struggle. Union membership swelled rapidly all over China.

The labor upheaval stirred by the general strike at Hong Kong was the handwriting on the wall for all Western employers in China. The commissioner of police of Shanghai's International Settlement warned grimly that no Western power in China could consider itself safe from the impending storm.

In Shanghai 20,000 women workers in twenty-four silk factories went out on strike, demanding a reduction of their working day from fourteen hours to ten and a wage increase of five cents per day. They were joined by other workers in the International Settlement for three days of street demonstrations with banners. The authorities arrested five leaders and hinted that they faced execution. Frightened, the women called off the strike. It was one of the few strikes of 1922 that was lost.

The Chinese Communists won adherents in cities throughout China by emphasizing workers' grievances in their first party manifesto. Their demands included ending the system of privileges for foreigners, votes for all Chinese, freedom of assembly and the right to strike, prohibition of child and woman labor, sanitary working conditions, and the repeal of laws permitting physical torture and executions.

The Hong Kong general strike opened the Kuomintang's eyes to the value of labor unions in aiding the struggle against Western imperialism. The party cooperated with the Communists in enlisting labor for this purpose. In 1924 the Kuomintang's door was officially opened to the Communists, who joined with Sun Yat-sen's party in a union that lasted for three years.

In some respects, the cataclysmic Chinese Revolution actually began in the ports of Hong Kong, on the day that 1,500 Chinese seamen decided they would no longer tolerate the injustices forced upon them, and risked everything to demand their human rights.

7

"JEWS? WHAT JEWS? I SEE ONLY DANISH CITIZENS!"

Denmark's Fight for Freedom

In Copenhagen, even in the wintry March of 1940, the fun-loving Danes were too busy enjoying life in their sports halls, theaters, restaurants, dance halls, night clubs, and beer halls to think much about the crazy man of Germany beyond their borders.

No attention was paid to the two Germans in civilian clothes who arrived in the lovely city by train. They strolled around the streets and docks for several days, then returned to Berlin. One was General Kurt Himer, chief of staff of a special Nazi task force. The other was a major, Himer's battalion commander. Their visit to Copenhagen was a reconnaissance mission.

Adolph Hitler had decided to invade Denmark and use it for air bases in his war against Great Britain.

A Dutch military attaché in Berlin learned of the imminent invasion and immediately informed the Danish naval attaché, who flashed a warning to Copenhagen. But King Christian X of Denmark refused to believe that the Nazis would outrage world opinion by attacking neutral Denmark. With its thousand-year history as a free nation, the serene little country seemed as immune to the danger of invasion as Switzerland.

Dismissing the warning as a rumor, the king went off to a performance at Copenhagen's Royal Theater.

One hour before dawn on April 9, 1940, the Danish foreign minister was awakened and handed a note brought by a German envoy. It was an ultimatum from the Nazi government. Alleging an Anglo-French plot to occupy Denmark and Norway, the note demanded that the Danish government instantly accept "the protection of the Reich."

German troops were even now landing in Denmark. Unlike the already invaded Norwegians—whose large, distant, and mountainous terrain made guerrilla warfare possible—the Danes had no hope of resistance. Their flat country could be quickly overrun by Nazi tanks. The Danes offered no suicidal defense, although as a matter of national pride the Danish army attempted a few half-hearted skirmishes. By breakfast time the invasion was a fait accompli.

The next day, Danish students issued a call for resistance. Seventeen-year-old Arne Sejr and his school friends distributed copies of a leaflet called "The Commandments for Danes." It read in part: "1. You must not go to work in Germany or Norway. 2. You must work badly for the Germans. . . . 4. You must spoil their production machines and tools. . . . 6. You must delay all German transports. . . . 8. You must not buy or trade with the Nazis. . . . 10. You must defend every person persecuted by the Germans. JOIN THE FIGHT FOR DENMARK'S FREEDOM!"

Sejr and his friends organized a student resistance movement, which published an underground newspaper which was soon being read in every part of Denmark.

The Danes had a long tradition of democratic attitudes and institutions, with a stubborn insistence on freedom of speech and press. Their society was based on the conviction that each citizen would be stronger for cooperating with his fellows. Now, many patriots began joining hands to resist the Nazi occupation.

Hoping to win Danish cooperation, the Germans were careful at first to keep up the fiction of Danish sovereignty. The Danish government was permitted to remain, with no changes in the laws, courts, or police force. The Germans did not even prevent a scheduled election, hoping that the Danes would be pragmatic and elect Fascists. The Danes did not.

Many citizens were stunned at first, unable to believe what had happened to their country. They felt helpless and fearful of the Gestapo, which kept a sharp eye out for the smallest token of resistance. But as the months passed, the shock wore off and the Danes felt a need to regain their self-respect.

The Allies were at first in no position to help. The Danish resistance movement started as a homemade effort. By 1943, however, the British set up a special operation to parachute weapons, explosives, and other equipment to resistance forces in Denmark. Farmers in north Jutland would wait in fields at night with flashlights to guide airdrops. They would speedily gather and hide the parachuted material before German guards could arrive in trucks.

Danish agents were trained as saboteurs in England. Parachuted back to join the underground, they were concealed by farmers in barns, along with British Royal Air Force pilots who crashed in Denmark. Few were betrayed, despite the Nazi offer of a $3,000 reward to any Dane who disclosed the whereabouts of a saboteur or British airman.

When airdrops became increasingly dangerous, a new system was worked out. British planes would drop containers into the sea near the shore. The containers would sink to the bottom, releasing small buoys that rose to the surface to mark their location. Men of the resistance, disguised as fishermen, would row out to the buoys and retrieve the containers.

The most daring Danish resistance came from a group of 150 saboteurs known as BOPA. Led by Communists who had fought against Franco in Spain, they robbed Wehrmacht stores and Danish arsenals for arms and explosives. Those employed as demolition workers were able to requisition explosives from the German authorities. Some were used to blow up German ships, planes, and war factories.

BOPA and another Danish resistance group called *Holger Danske* committed over 1,000 acts of sabotage. In one combined action they blew up twenty Germany army oil dumps in Copenhagen simultaneously. Such sabotage spared Copenhagen the massive Allied bombing that would otherwise have been necessary. But the price was high. Almost all the resistance leaders were caught by the Germans and executed.

The sabotage of the Nazis was not just the work of a handful of daring militants but a movement of the Danish people. Loathing their conquerors, they eagerly welcomed every opportunity to strike a blow for freedom.

Danish laborers dumped pounds of sugar into the cement they mixed for German gun emplacements. The first time the guns were fired, the mounts crumbled. Copenhagen postmen tore up letters to the Gestapo from suspected informers. Farm carts, hearses, furniture vans, beer trucks, and logging vehicles delivered concealed explosives and weapons to resistance groups.

The Danish underground created a central news agency called Information, the only underground press service in any Nazi-occupied country. It provided news of the resistance to underground papers all over Denmark. Hunted down relentlessly, the agency was forced to change hiding places twenty-seven times.

Defying Nazi censorship, the resistance press published 600 underground newspapers during the war, circulating a total of 26 million copies. One paper was even printed in Braille. Editors were captured, tortured, and sometimes executed. But the resistance press continued to defy the Nazis from attics, caves, cellars, and office storerooms.

On August 23, 1943, editors of the regular Danish press were summoned by Dr. Werner Best, Nazi administrator in Denmark. "Every editor will be answerable for his life," he warned angrily, "for further attempts to poison the popular mind!"

Some resistance news dispatches were taped under German goods wagons crossing on the boat train to Sweden, which was a neutral country and served as a conduit for Danish underground messages to the Allies. Others were smuggled to Sweden in hollow pencils or fountain pens. German pilots unwittingly carried resistance dispatches which workers had placed inside the wooden chocks used to brake the wheels.

The publishers of illicit newspapers also secretly produced hundreds of books banned by the Nazis. One unique publication was a "cookbook" giving recipes for concocting and using explosives. Some contraband volumes were distributed by students, other by booksellers who hid them in store cellars.

Mogens Staffeldt's bookshop in Dagmarhus was a key meeting place for the resistance. Whenever it was not felt safe to meet there, Staffeldt would arrange the books in his window in a certain way to warn Danes in the underground.

The resistance was also aided by Danes in the civil service.

Policemen passed Nazi security information to BOPA and *Holger Danske* so that saboteurs could avoid traps being set for them. Fire brigades, municipal engineering offices, and harbor bureaus supplied the resistance with information that helped saboteurs strike targets at the most vulnerable times and place explosives to do the greatest damage.

Out of the Danish population of 4,280,000, a bare 1 percent could be induced by the Nazis to join the Waffen SS. This handful of traitors feared daily for their lives. The resistance had special squads to eliminate collaborators and informers.

On August 25, 1943, the largest exhibition hall in Copenhagen was scheduled to become a German army barracks. The day before, Danish workmen carried in what was apparently a crate of Tuborg beer. A few minutes later the hall blew up in a tremendous explosion. The infuriated Nazis decreed that any Dane caught with explosives or firearms would be killed instantly.

Carlo Christensen, an official in the Ministry of Foreign Affairs in Copenhagen, was shocked when a policeman tipped him off in September that in a few days the Nazis would begin rounding up Danish Jews for German concentration camps.

There were less than 8,000 Jews—1,500 of them half-Jewish—in Denmark. Racial or religious prejudice was unknown. The Danes considered it barbaric to discriminate against anyone because of the circumstances of birth.

Christensen, a member of the resistance, quickly passed the warning along to Hans Hedtoft, the Danish prime minister. Hedtoft went to see the head of the Jewish community. Plans were made to help as many Jews as possible escape to Sweden. On October 1 the persecution began.

At 9:34 P.M. all phones were cut off to prevent Danes from

warning Jewish friends. Jews who had not fled their homes were dragged out by the Gestapo, tied together like animals, and driven along the streets. Some were jammed aboard a transport in the harbor, others loaded onto a train of cattle cars which stopped at town after town to pick up more Jews.

Some despairing Danish Jews committed suicide.

The Danes were thoroughly outraged. The German administration in Copenhagen had assured Danish authorities that Danish Jews would not be persecuted. The resistance now rallied the whole nation in a full-scale rescue effort.

Before the Gestapo could spread its dragnet, Danish Jews were snatched to safety by neighbors and taxi drivers. They were hidden in hospitals, attics, cellars, churches, and other institutions. Children stood guard against surprise raids until concealed Jewish families could be spirited away to the docks. Danish customs boats, harbor patrol launches, police boats, freighters, and fishing trawlers took them aboard, hid them, and spirited them to safety in Sweden.

Danes who were caught sheltering Jews were arrested. Those apprehended in attempts to help Jews escape were shot and killed. These tactics did not deter the Danish people. The whole population joined in a gigantic secret operation to help their Jewish countrymen survive.

When Nazis burst into a church and discovered Jews hidden in the cellar, the Gestapo officer shouted angrily at the minister, "How dare you use a Christian church to hide Jews!"

"Jews?" the minister replied coldly. "What Jews? I see only Danish citizens!"

Jews hidden in hospitals were transported in Danish Red Cross ambulances. When stopped by German patrols, the drivers would explain that their passengers were lunatics being transferred from one asylum to another.

Twenty refugees aboard a small freighter were concealed in a room under the officer's mess covered by an almost invisible hatch. Arriving in Swedish waters, the ship was approached by a Swedish coast guard vessel. Its officer asked whether refugees were on board. He was told they were. He then grinned, "Have you got Danish beer?" He received both.

Danish pilots, who knew how to maneuver through the mined sea lanes, piloted German ships by day and operated resistance transports at night. They helped downed British airmen and wounded resistance agents, as well as Jews, escape to Sweden.

Risking torture and death, the Danes helped over 7,000 Jews slip through the Nazi net. The enraged Gestapo was able to seize only a few hundred. To save face, it issued a manifesto declaring that the "criminal element" of the Danish population had now been removed. Indignant Danes —including the commander of the Danish army, prominent churchmen, scientists, artists, industrialists, and merchants— courageously joined in publicly denouncing this slander of the Jews as a lie. The Germans glumly said no more about the Danish Jews.

The Danish government, no longer willing to remain in office under the Nazi occupation, resigned and went underground to work with the resistance as the Freedom Council.

On Midsummer Night 1944, an occasion which the Danes celebrate much as Americans celebrate the Fourth of July, the German blackout was violated by an outbreak of fireworks and skyrockets from Copenhagen's beloved Tivoli amusement park. It was really a joyous celebration of the opening of the Second Front, which the Danes saw as the beginning of the end for the Nazis.

The public address system in the Town Hall tower played "Tipperary" and other Allied songs. Crowds in the huge Town Hall Square cheered and laughed. A flood of leaflets were circulated hailing the defiant spirit of "fighting Denmark."

Infuriated, the Nazis dynamited the Tivoli. An 8:00 P.M. curfew was imposed and was promptly violated by hundreds of thousands of Danes, who took evening strolls around Copenhagen's suburbs. Several hundred were arrested. Sixty mocked the Germans by claiming they had been "sleepwalking."

To enforce the curfew, German patrols began riding through crowds firing light machine guns. Over 200 Danes were wounded, and several killed. Enraged Danes tore up paving stones and built street barricades topped by the Danish flag. They set huge bonfires in which they burned oil-soaked swastikas and pictures of Hitler. Some of the most defiant rebels were incensed old women.

The resistance called a general strike. Every shop, factory, and office in Copenhagen shut down. Citizens in Esbjerg, Aalborg, and Odense joined the strike. Dr. Werner Best declared martial law. He would bring the Danes to their knees, he vowed furiously, or exterminate them all.

Copenhagen was ringed by Panzer divisions. Thousands in the resistance began escaping through the city's sewers. Danish police were ordered to round them up. When the entire police force refused, they were sent to concentration camps. Some police escaped and joined the resistance.

The Freedom Council refused to call off the general strike until the Nazis sullenly agreed to order its hated Schalburg Corps out of the city, stop shooting people, and end the curfew.

Danish saboteurs gave the Germans no rest. Three Danish

frogmen placed explosives under four German warships in Copenhagen harbor and blew them to pieces. Other saboteurs blew up German troop trains. British Field Marshal Bernard Montgomery credited them with having stopped every Danish train for two crucial weeks during the Battle of the Bulge, preventing the Germans from getting reinforcements to the Western Front.

The Danes also drove the Germans frantic by coordinated slowdowns in factories producing vital war materials. "The Germans could find no effective way of dealing with it," noted British military expert Basil Liddell Hart. "At intervals, exasperated, they insisted on the removal of some particular administrator whom they suspected of such practises—but he bequeathed his policy and plans to his successor."

Slowdowns on the job, Hart declared, were much more baffling and frustrating to the Nazis than open defiance, and could be sustained for much longer. Field Marshal Montgomery also praised the Danish resistance as "second to none," calling it a solid contribution to the defeat of the Nazis.

Perhaps nothing damaged German morale more than the Danish weapon of ridicule. The Nazis expected and could shrug off hate, but they could not endure being laughed at. According to celebrated Danish entertainer Victor Borge, the Danes began to knit and wear little woollen "beanie" caps with the British Royal Air Force red, white, and blue rosette insignia. The Nazis felt compelled to issue an absurd order forbidding any Dane to wear a red, white, and blue beanie.

One bookstore displayed English books with a sign reading: *Think of the future—learn English*. When the Nazis ordered the English books replaced by German volumes, the proprietor complied with a new sign: *Learn German—while there is still time*. The angry Nazis then insisted that his window display glorify the Rome-Berlin Axis. So the proprietor displayed pictures of Hitler and Mussolini, and between them placed a famous book by Victor Hugo—*Les Miserables.*

Sly wit at the Nazis' expense heartened as well as amused Danes. Such acts of defiance helped to unite the Danish nation against its oppressors, encouraging similar acts of mockery. On one newspaper kiosk Nazis were enraged to find that a Dane had scrawled: *To hell with Hitler!* Underneath, a second line of graffiti declared: *Sorry, I don't want him. (signed) the Devil.*

The Danes were not afraid to show open contempt for the Nazis. Danish girls refused to date Germans. People refused to smile or nod at them. Glum Nazi troops got the message.

The Nazis were often outwitted by clever Danes in the resistance. Once a ship bringing in a cargo from Sweden was boarded by German inspection officials. One demanded of the Danish captain, "What do you have in these butter crates?"

Grinning sarcastically, the captain replied, "Well, this one here is full of machine guns, and that one full of ammunition."

"You will not be impertinent!" snapped the Nazi, and went on to inspect the rest of the cargo. The "butter" crates of guns and ammunition for the resistance were not opened.

The Nazis sought to smash the resistance by beating and torturing suspects for information. Ruth Philipsen of the Freedom Council knew the whereabouts and activities of every member. Captured, she kept silent even when the Gestapo beat her, yanked her hair, put thumb screws on her fingers, and threatened to kill her. Most suspects who refused to talk were shot.

The Nazi in charge of murdering Danish resistance members was Alfred Naujocks of the S.S.-Gestapo. He caught

and killed 3,000 of the 30,000 active members of the underground. And on Hitler's express orders, for every Nazi soldier
killed by the resistance, five innocent Danes were shot.

But no amount of terror intimidated the imaginative resistance, whose members and supporters came from every walk
of Danish life. Danes in the underground undertook to destroy the municipal airdrome at Aalborg, the biggest German
installation in that city. The task was forbidding: The airdrome was thoroughly guarded, and every Danish worker
entering it was searched.

The resistance developed a unique scheme. Danish airdrome workers began bringing their lunch in paper-covered
boxes. After a while these were taken for granted and not in-
spected. Gradually some of the boxes were used to smuggle
in small plastic high explosive or incendiary bombs with delayed fuses. These were stored in clothing lockers until more
than fifty had been accumulated. Then, at a given signal during a lunch break, three men slipped from hangar to hangar
placing the bombs in planes, oil dumps, and tool sheds.

One man aroused suspicion and was arrested at a time
when he had no bombs on him. He was taken off for ques-
tioning. The other Danish workers were anxious that he
might break under torture and reveal the plan.

The following dawn the time fuses began to go off. Blasts
blew up one part of the airdrome after another. In a few
minutes the whole complex was reduced to a shambles of exploded planes and burning debris.

At almost every station on Denmark's rail lines, workers cooperated with the resistance. When they received coded tele-
phone messages alerting them that trains carrying German
troops were expected to pass, the workers would notify the
nearest sabotage group. Rails would be blown up to derail
or delay the train. Repeated on a large scale all over Den-

mark, these tactics severely hampered German troop movements.

In March 1945, when the Allies speeded toward Berlin, the Danish resistance sought to bottle up German shipping in Copenhagen harbor. One night Danish naval students on tugs towed an old, unused freighter into the harbor. They sank it so that it blocked the exit of a new German minesweeper which had been brought in to clear the harbor of sonic mines sown by Allied aircraft. The tugs then escaped to Sweden.

Three Copenhagen pilot boats sailed past a German patrol on the pretext of guiding an incoming German convoy into port. They kept right on going until they reached Sweden. Other Danish harbor pilots vanished into the underground. No one was left to maneuver German ships through the thickly sown minefields. German shipping was badly paralyzed at the moment it most needed mobility.

On May 7, 1945, from his headquarters on the Danish frontier, German Admiral Karl Doenitz radioed instructions to German General Alfred Jodl at General Eisenhower's headquarters in Reims to sign a document of unconditional surrender.

The long nightmare was over for the occupied countries.

When British military units arrived in Copenhagen on May 4, they were greeted by enthusiastic crowds. That night candles flamed in windows all over Denmark to celebrate the country's liberation.

Resistance workers came into the open wearing red, white, and blue armbands. They arrested German officers, seized and jailed collaborators, and released patriots from prison. The Freedom Council came out of the underground to take part in a new, postwar government.

The Jews of the world thanked the brave and humanitarian Danish people for having saved so many Jewish lives.

"It was not the work alone of the many Danish fishermen who took a large number of refugees to Sweden," said Carlo Christensen, who became cultural counselor of the Danish embassy in Washington, "nor was it the work exclusively of the members of the resistance movement. It was in a sense the work of a whole nation—impossible without the cooperation of people from every level of the population and of the Swedish who opened their doors to the refugees."

This was also true of the Danish struggle for human rights, in which the whole nation had played a valuable role in helping to end the Nazi darkness that had fallen across Denmark and all of Europe.

8

THE BURNING SPEAR

Kenyatta's Struggle for Kenya's Independence

A state of emergency was declared by the British governor of Kenya, Sir Evelyn Baring, in October 1952. Mau Mau terrorists were raiding the lush farms of white settlers. Crops were set afire, farms burned, cattle destroyed, and natives who cooperated with the British were assassinated.

Six top Kikuyu leaders of the nationalist Kenya African Union (KAU) were seized in midnight police raids. One of those suspected of being the brains behind the Mau Mau uprising was Jomo "Burning Spear" Kenyatta. An indignant white settler described him as "that evil-eyed, hard-drinking, wenching, bloody-minded terrorist."

Kenyatta greeted the police by holding out his hands for their cuffs. "What took you so long, gentlemen?" he asked dryly. Warned of his danger by the Kikuyu tribal grapevine, he had scorned flight in favor of trusting to the justice of the British courts.

Kenyatta had steadfastly denied any ties to the Mau Mau underground. But he had repeatedly warned Kenya's white government against continuing to deny his people their human rights, and he had been organizing the Kikuyu to de-

mand these rights in their own country. By refusing to negotiate with African moderates like himself, the colonial government had made it inevitable that more and more black
Kenyans would turn to the violent Mau Mau.

The British secretly flew Kenyatta to a desert outpost in
the north of Kenya. Almost 300 minor Kikuyu leaders were
also rounded up. The government was taking no chances on
a mass uprising to liberate the Kikuyu leader.

Six battalions of the King's Rifles were added to the Lan-
cashire Fusiliers, as armored cars fanned all over Kikuyuland. The British government had declared war on a tribal
society.

The Mau Mau accepted the challenge, forming the Land
Freedom Army in the dense forests. Thousands of Kikuyu
flocked to join them. They swore a fierce oath: "When the
red-buck horn is blown, if I leave a European farm without
killing the owner, may this oath kill me!" One Mau Mau
leader told his followers, "We used to be the meat and the
white were the knives. But now *we* are the knives, and the
whites are the meat!"

Bands of Mau Mau burst into white farmers' houses, decapitated black servants, and hacked settlers and their families to death. The government retaliated by raiding Kikuyu
villages, flogging and torturing some suspects, and shooting
others. Thousands of Kikuyu families were driven out of
their homes and exiled in concentration camps.

The trial of Jomo Kenyatta in December 1952 attracted
the world's attention. The crucial issue was the rights of Africans in their own country versus the rights of the foreign
government that ruled them without their consent. British
Colonial Secretary Oliver Lyttelton called for severe punishment of Kenyatta and the outlawing of KAU, which he
blamed for Mau Mau terrorism.

"We disagree profoundly," replied two British Labor party MPs, Fenner Brockway and Leslie Hale, "Mau Mau is an ugly and brutal form of extreme nationalism. It is based on frustration. Frustration brings bitterness, and bitterness brings viciousness." Outlawing KAU, they argued, "would intensify bitterness and spread a feeling among Africans that the government is using the crimes of the Mau Mau to strike at legitimate African rights."

Instead of trying Kenyatta in the limelight of Nairobi, the Kenyan government set his trial in a remote little desert town that was without a railroad, telephones, or hotel facilities. Brought from England by KAU, Kenyatta's defense counsel, Denis N. Pritt, protested the "gross, cruel, deliberate injustices worked upon me by the government of Kenya in insisting on having this trial up here." He also charged that his phone in the town where he stayed had been tapped and his mail opened.

Later it was proved that some witnesses against Kenyatta had been bribed to perjure themselves. Kenyatta's rights were so abused in court that Pritt cabled Labor members in Parliament, advising them that a fair trial was impossible.

The bitter court fight went on for five months.

Kenyatta had grown up as a shepherd boy in the White Highlands, the fertile farmlands of the 2 million Kikuyu who made up a fifth of Kenya's black population. He watched white British settlers take over these lands. The immigrants developed large prosperous farms, while the Kikuyu struggled to raise enough to feed themselves on tiny plots of the poorest land.

In 1906 the Colonists' Association passed a Masters' and Servants' Ordinance giving white settlers the right to punish any native who refused to work on their farms for what amounted to serfs' wages. Three Kikuyu who resisted were publicly flogged in front of the Nairobi courthouse.

Kenyatta was outraged by the offenses against his people. Kikuyu were beaten or whipped if they were slow in responding to a white person's summons, or if they failed to tip their hats in respect. Drunken white men sometimes fired guns at Kikuyu's feet. Even elderly black men were called "boy" or "monkey." No blacks or East Indian shopkeepers were permitted in the hotels, restaurants, and churches of Nairobi and Mombasa. Only whites could serve on the Legislative Council that governed Kenya.

Kikuyu grievances about the land received unexpected support from the new undersecretary of state for the colonies in London, Winston Churchill. He warned the Council to heed Kikuyu complaints, declaring, "After all, it's *their* Africa."

Ignoring Churchill, the Legislative Council imposed a heavy hut tax on the Kikuyu. Many could not pay it because they were not allowed to grow coffee or other cash crops. More and more were forced to leave their tribal villages to work for starvation wages on the white settlers' big farms. Taxed almost half a million dollars in 1913, the Kikuyu received in return not a single public school in which to educate their children.

Two years later the Council passed a Crown Land Ordinance. It expropriated "all land occupied by the African tribes of the Colony," making legal ownership possible only for white Britons. At one stroke, black Kenyans became tenant farmers on their own lands. White farmers seized 16,000 square miles of choice grazing land owned by the Kikuyu tribe communally.

By 1919 thousands of Kikuyu had been thrown off their farms and dumped onto reservations. These thinly disguised concentration camps were divided into tiny garden plots. Some on the reservation died of starvation. Others fled to slum shacks in the cities to compete for paltry wages as servants or laborers.

Kenyatta quickly realized that he could not fight this system without an education that would enable him to enter the white man's world to speak for his people. He attended a mission school where he learned to read and write English.

After finishing at the mission school, he took a job as a clerk for public works in Nairobi, where he was chosen to be spokesman for the Kikuyu, protesting the Crown Land Ordinance before the Nairobi Supreme Court.

"The government does not appreciate that in the Kikuyu religion our soil is considered sacred," he argued. "You must understand that is the kinship bond that unites our families, the foundation rock on which our whole tribal economy is built. The government is taking away not only our livelihood, but our whole Kikuyu way of life!"

When the court turned a deaf ear, Kenyatta joined a militant group of young blacks which became known as the Kikuyu Central Association (KCA). It sought to recover the lost Kikuyu lands, place Africans on the Legislative Council, compel the building of schools for blacks, end the hut tax, and stop the European exploitation of black labor.

Kenyatta crusaded ceaselessly—traveling on foot, bike, and motorcycle to wherever there were groups of blacks to proselytize. The huge, spectacular figure in a cowboy hat with a beaded felt band, short-sleeved khaki jacket, beaded belt, riding breeches, and brown boots was under constant surveillance by the police. Kenyatta was marked for future arrest as "a dangerous agitator."

In 1925 the Church of Scotland Missions ruled that Kikuyu parents who would not pledge to keep their children out of tribal coming-of-age rites would not be permitted to send them to mission school, the only source of education in Kenya.

"First they take our lands," Kenyatta cried indignantly, "and now they want to destroy our people's sacred customs!"

He said later, "Missionaries . . . did not understand the value of the African custom, and many of them tried to stamp out some of the customs without knowing the part they play in the life of the Kikuyu. . . . They upset the life of the people."

He credited the missionaries with providing education and medical treatment for blacks, but felt that their primary aim was to train and control skilled black labor for the benefit of the white settlers.

Kenyatta decided that his people should control their own education by building Kikuyu schools, as well as a training college to provide teachers for these schools. His agitation led thousands to Kikuyu to boycott the mission schools and to contribute their labor and meager earnings to a new Kikuyu Independent School Association (KISA). Soon the first schools in Kenya run by blacks opened their doors.

Kenyatta gave up his government job to become general secretary of the KCA in 1928. Traveling around Kikuyuland, he held grievance meetings and raised funds for both the KCA and KISA. He began a KCA newspaper in the Kikuyu language, *Muigwithania*. The first paper published by natives in East Africa, it incited mass protests against the Crown Land Ordinance, beggarly pay, miserable housing, and bad working conditions.

The white settlers were quick to react. The Native Authority Ordinance forbade KCA organizers to collect money "without permits." Africans were forbidden to carry weapons, although many Europeans wore side arms. Under penalty of two-year jail sentences, no KCA meetings were allowed without permission of local government-appointed chiefs.

The East Indian storekeepers of Kenya were also discriminated against. Impressed by Kenyatta's struggle against the white settlers, they paid him to go to London to plead the case for a new Kenyan constitution that would give all the colony's minorities a voice in government. Kenyatta spent eighteen months in Europe publicizing grievances against the Kenya Council.

The Colonial Secretariat in London refused to see him, but in 1931 he was permitted to testify before the Carter Kenya Land Commission set up to investigate Kikuyu complaints.

The University of Moscow offered Kenyatta a two-year scholarship, which he accepted. But he was too much of an individualist to embrace Communism.

Kenyatta returned to England to work and study at the School of Oriental and African Studies. He also took a post-graduate course in anthropology at the University of London. His thesis there was a study of Kikuyu tribal life. Published as a book, *Facing Mount Kenya*, it won international acclaim and called attention to the white settlers' attempts to stamp out the Kikuyu culture, which they did not understand.

Invited to lecture, Kenyatta told audiences, "Africans are not hostile to Western civilization as such, but they are put in an intolerable posiiton when the European invasion destroys the very basis of their old tribal way of life, yet offers them no place in the new society except as serfs."

The outbreak of World War II delayed Kenyatta's return to Kenya. His colleagues wrote him that the colonial government was using the war as a pretext for banning the KCA and other native political organizations. More and more Kikuyu had been removed from their villages to the reserves. The KCA had gone underground and was operating clandestinely.

Kenyatta wrote a pamphlet called *Kenya: Land of Conflict*, which warned the white settlers that if they persisted in rejecting peaceful reform, they would have to deal with violent revolution.

When the war was over, his friends urged him to come home and lead the postwar struggle for independence as head of a new organization they had formed, the Kenya African Union (KAU). So after a fifteen-year absence Kenyatta returned in September 1946 to a hero's welcome, which astonished him.

Huge crowds of Africans roared their acclaim. They fought to touch the bearded giant who had made their cause internationally famous, and had now come home to rescue them from bondage. Wherever he went, he was mobbed by enthusiastic people crying out the magic name: "Jomo! Jomo! Jomo Kenyatta!"

He was deeply moved. Becoming president of KAU, he set out on a new crusade to win human rights for his people. Taking stock of the changes the war had wrought in Kenya, Kenyatta found that the settlers had prospered enormously. They had received high prices for food supplied to the military, and their financial success was evident in the building boom in Nairobi. Huge investments by overseas banks and oil firms had rejuvenated the city with skyscrapers, beautiful wide avenues, and expensive villas. Mombasa had become a bustling international seaport.

But none of this wealth had improved life for black Africans. They continued to be robbed of their lands and transferred to the overcrowded reserves. The ghetto slums were

even more miserable than when Kenyatta had left. Poverty
and suffering were the lot of those who had been forced to
give up subsistence farming for new lives in the cities.

Black veterans who had served with distinction abroad in
the King's Africa Rifles had returned to unemployment and
squalor. Some were "lucky" enough to be offered pick-and-
shovel work at $5.60 a month. Those who demanded better
were flogged for impertinence. Many preferred to use their
military training to help them steal for a living.

All the tribes in Kenya had suffered, but the Kikuyu, the
proudest tribe, had endured the greatest hardships. A reporter for the American weekly the *Nation* interviewed one
of Kenyatta's followers, asking what KAU meant to black
Kenyans.

"The people are waking up suddenly," he replied. "They
want education so that they can participate in this new
world. They don't get it. They don't get jobs of any importance. They can't communicate very well. They are frustrated. So they turn their attention to politics, where they
can throw themselves around and seem to be doing something."

Kenyatta called a mass meeting at Njoro. Thousands of
Kenyans from all tribes came long distances on foot, in carts,
and on old buses to hear the words of the great Kikuyu
leader back from London. A magnetic speaker, Kenyatta
used flamboyant, dramatic gestures to excite his listeners,
who responded with applause and enthusiastic laughter.

"I do not want the Europeans to leave the country," Kenyatta declared, "but it is time they started to behave like
guests in our house. They came to us as strangers, and we
gave them hospitality, and then they claimed that the house
belonged to them."

The crowd roared its approval.

"We carried their women on our shoulders and drew them in rickshaws from Mombasa to Nairobi. . . . We sent our young men to sacrifice their lives to help the British fight and conquer Germany. The white officers were rewarded with farms on which to settle in our land, and loans with which to stock them. Our African soldiers were rewarded with the color bar and unemployment, although there had been no color bar to prevent our dying for Britain in the war!"

Government spies took down every word. They were flabbergasted when Kenyatta dared to add, "We must unite together in KAU and forget tribalism. We must not let the Europeans forget that the land they tread is ours. We should . . . educate our people as quickly as possible, so that they can take over the government of the country for us!"

The skies over Njoro were rent with the trilling cries reserved to honor a great leader. Mobs of black Kenyans struggled to get close enough to touch Kenyatta. Black spies hurried back to Nairobi to warn their masters.

The white rulers of Kenya decided not to arrest Kenyatta, for fear of precipitating the very revolution they dreaded. Instead, they kept him under observation.

Kenyatta zealously stumped the country and held mass meetings, some as large as 40,000 people. Speaking for KAU, he demanded that the legislature grant Africans the right to vote in local elections, abolish racial discrimination, and return the confiscated White Highlands to the Kikuyu.

This was too much for the hard-line white settlers, who insisted that Kenyatta be jailed or exiled at once. Did the Council realize that in Kenyatta's KISA schools, black children were taught that the African life-style was culturally superior to the European?

And KISA schools were rapidly multiplying. Spurred by Kenyatta, parents were selling land and cattle to build the schools and were even carrying heavy stones to construction sites themselves. The children helped by raising the roofs. Three hundred KISA schools were educating 60,000 black children and inculcating them with aspirations to independence.

In July 1947 membership in KAU was over 100,000, and Kenyatta called a series of strikes to compel the government to make economic concessions to black farmers and workers.

At the same time a new secret society led by disaffected, jobless Kikuyu criminals began its own struggle against the white settlers. Known only as Mau Mau, its members swore to kill whites and drive them out of Kenya. The white settlers found themselves faced with peaceful resistance on one hand, terrorism on the other.

The Legislative Council decided to get tough with the Kikuyu. The number forced out of villages onto reserves was stepped up sharply. By 1948, 1 million—half the tribe—had been crowded into reserves originally intended for less than a third that number. Kenyatta appealed to the dislocated Kikuyu to join KAU's peaceful crusade for education, self-improvement, and political action. Many did, but about 200,000 made their way into the forests to take the Mau Mau oath of vengeance.

The white Kenya Citizens Association accused Kenyatta of being the mastermind behind Mau Mau. When he denied it, he was challenged to call a mass meeting and openly denounce Mau Mau. Kenyatta agreed, provided the government would, at the same time, agree openly to some of KAU's demands for reform.

But the governor of Kenya, pressed by the angry white settlers, refused to make a single concession. Mau Mau was declared an outlaw movement, with heavy punishments decreed for any who gave or took the oath. Kenyatta was

stunned when the governor also suppressed KISA because of
its "connection with Mau Mau."

Kenyatta's speeches became more militant as he barn-
stormed around the country. Speaking at enormous rallies, he
excoriated the government for stubbornly refusing to yield
any human rights to the people whose land it ruled.

In February 1952 Mau Mau members began raiding farms
in the White Highlands. They destroyed livestock and killed
entire white families. The government struck back with full
military force. And Jomo Kenyatta was arrested as the alleged chief conspirator behind Mau Mau and spirited off to
a desert prison.

Such were the facts he testified to at the trial held in a
shabby schoolhouse in a remote Kenyan outpost.

The prosecution tried to label Kenyatta a Communist. He
denied the charge as nonsense. And if anyone were to blame
for Mau Mau, he declared, it was not KAU, but the Council.

"The government," he pointed out, "instead of joining with
us to fight Mau Mau, arrested all the leading members of
KAU, accusing them of being Mau Mau. . . . They have arrested thousands of people who would have been useful in
helping to put things right in the country. . . . What they
wanted to eliminate is the only political organization—KAU
—which fights constitutionally for the rights of the African
people!"

But he and the other KAU defendants were found guilty
and sentenced to seven years at hard labor in a bleak desert
post in northern Kenya. "We do not accept your findings,"
Kenyatta told the judge defiantly. "We have not received justice!"

News of the verdict swept through Kenya like heat lightning, arousing the people's wrath. Mau Mau heightened its

terrorist raids on white settlers. Fighting in Kenya intensified to the level of a civil war.

In prison camp Kenyatta was beaten, humiliated, overworked, and tortured. "I was just a mere convict, known by number, not by name," he later related. "I was told that that was one of the punishments—to deny me all the privileges that I had before. I was treated just like a common prisoner."

Prayers were said for him all over Kenya—in prison camps, on the crowded reserves, and in city slums. The governor of Kenya learned that a movement was under way to preserve Kenyatta's home as a Kikuyu shrine. The house was ordered burned and the land confiscated for use as an experimental farm.

But the Kenyan government failed to realize the extent to which Kenyatta's appeal to world opinion had aroused sympathy for him and his people. Growing pressure for his release and for an end to the brutal colonialism in Kenya came from all over the world. The Conservative government of Britain came under fire from the British Labor party for having soiled the reputation of British justice by permitting Kenyatta's persecution.

In April 1955 a paralyzing strike was organized on the docks of Mombasa by a young Kenyan leader, Tom Mboya. The strikers won a remarkable 33 percent increase in wages before they agreed to return to work.

The Council, shaken by all these developments, sought to pour oil on troubled waters. Almost 80,000 Kikuyu detained behind barbed wire on the reserves were released. The Council promised to investigate charges of police brutality, the use of slave labor in the farms of the White Highlands, and the arbitrary confiscation of Kikuyu lands.

In 1956 the war against the Mau Mau came to an end.

Over 11,000 blacks had been killed, 1,000 more hanged, and 3,000 captured. The government forces had lost 32 white civilians, 57 white soldiers, and 1,740 African loyalists. The cost of the civil war to the government was estimated at $200 million.

But by 1957 the handwriting was on the wall. Admonished by 10 Downing Street, the government was forced to recognize that concessions would have to be made to black nationalism. Tom Mboya warned of a new general strike if Africans were not allowed to vote in the May 1957 national election. The colonial government reluctantly agreed, but barred Kikuyu participation.

By refusing to enfranchise the largest and most educated Kenyan tribe, the government was able to keep the Council at least half-white. Kenya's 50,000 white settlers still exercised control over 5½ million Africans. Mboya demanded another fifteen seats for blacks on the Council.

Speaking before a cheering crowd of Africans, he told Europeans, "Your time is past. Get out of Africa!" He demanded that Kenyatta be immediately released to head a new black Kenyan government.

Mboya's cry was echoed all over the country: *"Uhuru na Kenyatta!"* ("Freedom and Kenyatta!") Militant young nationalists marched through the cities and villages in pro-Kenyatta demonstrations. A new political party was organized —the Kenya African National Union (KANU). Kenyatta was elected unanimously as president in absentia.

In April 1959 the government released Kenyatta from his desert prison camp, but held him in a remote village. To quiet the great outcry on his behalf, Kenyatta was allowed to live in a small cottage and receive government-censored newspapers.

Defending his continued detention, a government white

paper charged that Kenyatta had done "his utmost to conceal the savage and revolutionary Mau Mau movement behind a facade of nationalism."

Kenyatta accused the government of lying. "I was doing all I could to avoid violence," he insisted, "and in many cases I denounced violence in my political meetings. My denunciations were not given wide publicity because for one reason or another the government wanted to paint me . . . black in character. They tried to put all the evil things on me."

Kenya's chief tribal leaders came together in KANU to press for independence and Kenyatta's immediate release. Under intense pressure from world opinion and the London Foreign Office, the new governor of Kenya felt helpless to stop the democratic process, however much this angered diehard white settlers. He made a last desperate effort to split the African vote by secretly organizing a coalition of minority tribes into a rival organization to KANU. It bore a deliberately similar name to confuse voters—the Kenya African Democratic Union (KADU).

The first fully democratic national election in Kenya took place on February 28, 1961. The whole country seethed with excitement as Turkana tribeswomen of the far northwest in skins and claw necklaces flocked to the polls with the elegantly dressed wives of white settlers. Black Kenyans, thrilled at the prospect of finally having a voice in their own government, turned out in huge numbers. In his dusty village of confinement, Kenyatta waited tensely for the results that would determine his fate.

A roar of delight rose in Kenya as the news spread that KANU had won a sweeping victory. It had trounced the government-supported KADU by winning three times as many votes. As the majority party in Kenya, KANU was now entitled to form a new government under the governor. But the leaders of KANU refused to form a government without Jomo Kenyatta.

The governor rejected their demand that he be freed. Once Kenyatta was released, almost all black Kenya would unite solidly behind him. The days of power for the white settlers would be at an end. The governor's refusal sent a wave of anger through the country. Mau Mau members released from detention began swearing new oaths. A huge protest meeting was held. A speaker cried, "Africans were made beggars in their own country while Europeans farmed comfortably on the Highlands. These Europeans must have their farms taken from them! This is *our* country!"

The governor tried to thwart KANU by getting the leader of KADU to form a new government, supported by white members of the Legislative Council. All over Kenya a deafening roar of protest arose at this defiance of the election results. The leader of KADU warned the governor, "I will be unable to stay in office unless Kenyatta is freed immediately."

The governor consulted the British colonial secretary and was sternly told to order the release of the Kikuyu leader. Defeated, the governor finally gave in. He sent a police plane to bring Kenyatta home after seven years in exile.

At a welcome-home rally it seemed as though every black Kenyan in the country had jammed into Nairobi. Kenyatta was greeted with delirium. Drums thundered in celebration. Barefoot women danced joyfully, shrilling, "Kenyatta is home! Thank you, Jomo!"

He greeted them with one word: *"Uhuru!"* ("Freedom!")

Wherever he traveled, vast crowds surged to see and hear the symbol of the emerging new nation. He was showered with gifts of livestock and corn.

The white settlers schemed frantically with the governor

to keep British rule. The leader of KADU was allowed to promise that landless Africans would receive a million acres of white-held lands, and that qualified Africans could apply for better jobs. The governor sought to sidetrack Kenyatta from the movement for independence by appointing him minister of state for constitutional affairs and economic planning.

Accepting the post, Kenyatta accustomed himself to the trappings of power and bided his time. In 1963 he led KANU in vigorous parliamentary elections, scoring another sweeping victory over KADU. The people of Kenya had spoken decisively. And the world had heard. The governor now had no choice but to accept Jomo Kenyatta as the new prime minister of the colony.

British rule had become a technicality. At last power belonged to the people of Kenya. After great suffering, they had won their fight to be free and sovereign.

Kenyatta told the apprehensive white settlers, "We can all work together harmoniously to make this country great, and to show other countries in the world that different racial groups can live and work together. Become Africans in your hearts, and we will welcome you with open arms!" Then he cried out the Swahili slogan urging cooperation: "Harambee!"

The white farmers jammed into the hall were stunned for a moment. Then one after another rose. Sweeping aside the color barrier that had cursed Kenya for most of a century, they shouted in reply, "Harambee! Harambee!"

Black and white would make a fresh start together.

On December 11, 1963, the British Union Jack was hauled down in Kenya. The green, red, and black flag of the Republic of Kenya was hoisted to proclaim that human rights had been restored to all the people of the land.

9

"AVENGE THE DEAD!"

The Basque Battle
for Nationhood

"I don't want to have anything to do with Spain," said Juan Beistegui, a bicycle shop owner in Bilbao who had once been jailed for resistance activities. "I want complete separation. ... We do not accept the idea that anybody should make laws for us, the Basques. ... We do not want to impose our race and language on anybody else; we just want them for ourselves."

The Basques are one of the oldest known races in Europe. A non-Latin people of uncertain origin, they have had their own language and culture for at least 5,000 years. They wear rakish berets, which men never doff in public, play the wild game of *pelote* (jai alai), and do leaping dances to the tuneless music of drums and ebony flutes.

A round-faced, stocky people, some 750,000 live in four provinces of northern Spain—Vizcaya, Guipúzcoa, Álava and Navarre. Another 150,000 Basques live across the border in France.

Most Basques today live in big industrial centers. About one in five is a shepherd living in a whitewashed farmhouse or stone hut, or a fisherman whose home perches between sheer cliffs above stormy bays. Because these four provinces are economically important to Spain, the government has taken a dim view of granting the Basques full autonomy.

The government props up its shaky economy by heavily taxing the Basque iron ore, shipping, and timber industries. Yet it spends less than 5 percent of these taxes on the Basque region. Bilbao—a center of shipbuilding, steel production, and banking—has some of the worst slums in Europe.

For centuries the Basques managed to keep successive invading armies of Carthaginians, Romans, Visigoths, and Franks out of their region of the Pyrenees Mountains. During the Middle Ages the kings of Navarre recognized the Basques as a separate race. Granting them exemption from military service with the Spanish, they also forbade Spanish troops to enter the Basque provinces.

For the next 800 years the Basques were allowed, to a great extent, to govern themselves. Their assemblies met under a huge oak tree in Guernica that came to be regarded as a symbol of Basque liberty.

In 1528 Andrew Navagero, a Venetian historian who traveled through the Pyrenees, noted how different the Basques were from Spaniards. "The people of this country are very gay and are quite the opposite of the Spaniards, who can do nothing save gravely," he wrote. "These people are always laughing, joking and dancing, both men and women."

In 1839 the Spanish government abolished Basque rights. Forced to accept "foreign" rule, the Basques resisted every attempt to Hispanicize them. A fiercely proud, independent people, they clung stubbornly to their own distinctive culture and language.

Basques who lived on the French side of the border were less alienated. The French government wisely permitted them to practice their culture, and granted them basic free-

doms as French citizens. But whenever Basques on either
side of the border were asked whether they were Spanish or
French, they replied firmly, "Neither—we are Basque!"

They insisted upon speaking their difficult, unique language, *Euskara,* which is little known outside Basque country. In the late 1930's the Francoist government tried to
stamp out the language and compel the Basques to speak
Spanish.

That would have made it easier for the Guardia Civil, Fascist Spain's paramilitary security police, to smoke out subversive plots against the regime. But the Basques clung stubbornly to their language as another way to defy their Spanish
overlords.

In 1932 the Spanish monarchy had come to an end when
Republicans won an election victory. Seeking Basque support, the Republicans had promised restoration of the ancient Basque rights abolished in 1839. When Generalissimo
Francisco Franco led a Fascist army revolt against the government in 1936, he denounced the promise to the Basques
as a blow to Spain's "sacred unity."

The Republican Madrid government (also known as the
Loyalists) kept its promise by granting the Basques autonomy. The Basques promptly formed an independent republic
and organized their own militia units to oppose Franco. As
the Fascist insurgents swept across Spain, they met their
fiercest resistance in Basque country.

The pope asked Franco to recognize Basque autonomy.
The Vatican was embarrassed by a civil war between such
devoutly Catholic factions. Franco refused and demanded
that the pope denounce the Basques and the Basque priests
supporting them. The Vatican simply exhorted Spanish
Catholics not to support communism. Since Franco accused

the Loyalists of being Communists, he claimed the blessings of the Church on his crusade against the government and the Basques.

Not all Basques supported the Republican government. A minority believed Franco propaganda about the "Reds" who were "anti-Christ." These pro-Franco Basques, or Requetés, chose to fight with the Fascist forces. Tragically, priests fought against priests, sons against fathers, brothers against brothers.

Franco opened his campaign to capture the Basque country in March 1936. German and Italian air forces lent to Franco by Hitler and Mussolini bombed Basque towns, communications, and military positions. Francoist General Emilio Mola grew incensed at the impassioned resistance of Basques in Vizcaya Province.

"If they do not surrender immediately," he threatened on March 31, 1937, "I will raze all Vizcaya to the ground beginning with the industries of war. I have the means to do so."

Marching behind a shield of incendiary bombs dropped by Condor Legion planes, his forces advanced to within ten miles of Guernica. Opposing them was a Basque army of blue-overalled students, mechanics, and peasants. Led by a handful of regular officers, they were armed only with ancient rifles. Their artillery consisted of homemade bombs made up of three sticks of dynamite in tomato cans, with fuses lit by a burning cigarette.

"We went on fighting because there was nothing else to do," Basque sergeant Aristarco Yoldi said later, "and because we believed in ourselves, and because we lived on hopes of help coming from abroad. We could fight well against the Moors, the Italians, and the Legionnaires, for we knew the mountain trails better than they did. The Requetés were our worst enemies; they spoke our language, and they knew the trails as well as we did. They could infiltrate into our lines."

Heavy shelling and aerial bombardment forced the Basques to fall back. They suffered terrible casualties trying to bury their dead. Despite the hopelessly unequal battle, the Basques fought tenaciously, and even when the enemy captured Crucetas, the Basques retook it three times.

But their cause grew increasingly hopeless as their food and ammunition ran out. The remaining defenders staggered about from lack of sleep. Franco's forces captured 200 Basque officers. In defiance of the rules of warfare, the prisoners were deliberately shot in groups.

On market day, April 26, 1937, wave after wave of German Condor Legion bombers suddenly appeared over the pine hills of Guernica. They dove down on the crowded marketplace, dropping sticks of explosives and machine-gunning people who were fleeing in horror to the hills. The bombardment continued until the town was leveled. Between 2,000 and 3,000 Basque civilians were killed or wounded. Then fire bombs were dropped on the city.

Guernica burned for three days.

"Women, children and old men were falling in heaps, like flies," related one Basque priest, Father Alberto de Onaindia, "and everywhere we saw lakes of blood. . . . We were completely incapable of believing what we saw. During the first hours of the night it was a most horrifying spectacle; men, women and children were wandering through the woods in search of loved ones. In most cases they found only their bullet-riddled bodies."

The indiscriminate bombing of civilians in an open town made Guernica an international symbol of Fascist savagery. Worldwide denunciation of Franco, Hitler, and Mussolini reached such proportions that Franco desperately sought to label the wanton destruction of Guernica as the "exaggeration" of an American correspondent. Franco's propaganda chief even accused the Republicans of firing Guernica themselves so that they could blame the Fascists.

But a subsequent impartial investigation revealed that the Condor Legion's Stuka dive-bombers had carried out the attack on Guernica at Franco's request, in order to destroy the Basque people's morale and terrorize them into surrender.

The destruction of Guernica did lead to the collapse of Basque resistance, assuring Franco of dictatorial control of all Spain. But the horror of his act was recorded for posterity in a world-famous painting, *Guernica*, by Picasso, a memorial to Basque martyrdom.

Franco lost no time in placing Spanish civil and military governors in all four Basque provinces, and encouraging Spaniards to migrate to these regions and Hispanicize them. All forms of Basque nationalism were banned. It became a punishable offense to speak *Euskara* in schools, on the street, on radio, or TV. No books could be published in *Euskara*.

In 1949 Franco fell overboard while fishing from his yacht in Basque waters. He was rescued by a boy fisherman, who received a medal and a gift of money. Returning home, the boy proudly recounted his feat to his father, a secret member of the Basque National Party (PNV) pledged to home rule.

"You young jackass!" his father roared. "Why didn't you let him drown? Heaven will never send us such a chance again!"

Suppressing labor unions, Franco severely punished workers who sought to strike. In 1958 Basque priest Carlos Martin Castaneda defied Franco by preaching a sermon defending strikers, and taking up a collection for them.

"Though I exceed my pastoral functions," he declared, "I

cannot fail to voice a protest from this sacred place . . . against the oppressions, violences and brutalities to which our various brother laborers have been subjected." He was suspended and transferred to a monastery.

In 1960 more than forty Basque priests signed a letter denouncing police brutality and press censorship, and demanding human rights for their parishioners. The letter was suppressed. Each signer was reprimanded by Franco-appointed church prelates, who warned the priests of suspension.

In 1962 Basque workers at Bilbao laid down their tools, demanding a living wage and the right to join free unions. Their defiance sparked a wave of strikes throughout the mining regions. Supported by their local priests, the Basque workers held firm despite arrests and firings.

Franco rushed reinforcements of the Guardia Civil to the northern provinces. Proclaiming a state of emergency, he suspended all civil rights. Spain's leading Roman Catholic magazine, *Ecclesia*, stunned the dictator by coming out in favor of the strikers. The Church was becoming increasingly disenchanted with Francoism.

"The Church always speaks the truth," declared the abbot of Montserrat. "If this truth is not welcome to those that govern, then it is up to them to change things."

Franco ordered rough treatment of all clergy supporting the Basque strikers. Three priests were arrested. But firm church pressure finally compelled Franco to accede to some of the strikers' demands. To save face, he fired his minister of labor, blaming him for provoking the strike.

The illegal Basque National Party (PNV) was a unifying symbol of Basque resistance, but its aging leaders were often ineffective in achieving Basque goals. In 1962 militant young Basques formed a new secret underground movement called the *Euskadi et Askatusana* ("Basqueland and Liberty"), and

soon known as ETA. To put spine into the struggle for
Basque autonomy, ETA organized illegal factory unions,
which tried to win concessions from Franco by use of
the strike threat. But this strategy was considered too tame
by a small number of members. Calling themselves ETA V
and ETA VI, they set out to match the Spanish dictator
terror for terror.

Although both factions of ETA used different tactics, they
pursued the same goals—political, economic, and cultural
freedom for the four Spanish and three French Basque provinces, which they wanted to form the United States of Spain.
In the public mind the two ETA factions gradually became
indistinguishable.

Members of the ETA hunted by the Guardia Civil were
frequently forced to flee Spain. Often they would wait for
hours neck-deep in the Bidassoa River separating Spain from
France, until darkness permitted them to slip across the
guarded border. Others crawled through snow-covered
mountain passes, guided by owllike whistles from their con-
tacts on the French side.

In France they would be taken to one of a string of sanctu-
aries in Bayonne or the nearby resort of Biarritz. Over 700 of
the 1,000 or so Spanish Basques exiled in France were ETA
members. Many risked death not only by returning across
the border, but also by participating in commando raids.

Franco repeatedly pressured the French government to
deny Basques sanctuary. The French Basques argued that
their Spanish cousins had "the right to live freely" in France
without being "hindered" by the authorities. When French
police sought to round up suspected ETA terrorists, young
French Basques protested by staging sit-in hunger strikes in
churches throughout southwestern France.

Most ETA militants were taught guerrilla warfare at secret

bases in Spain. Some were trained and armed by terrorist groups in Libya, Ireland, and Algeria. What set ETA commandos apart from other terrorists was that the Basques usually took care not to engage in indiscriminate acts of violence. Their targets were banks, police stations, and radio stations. The victims they attacked were usually Spanish government officials, big business supporters of Franco, or police known to have tortured political prisoners.

The Guardia Civil was now concentrated more heavily in the Basque provinces than anywhere else in Spain, ostensibly to keep down violence. Their real purpose was to intimidate the Basques, who regarded them with thinly disguised hatred. Basque girls refused to go out with them. No Basque spoke to them unless it was absolutely necessary.

In 1968 one ETA group assassinated two police officials, one of them the head of the Guipuzcoa secret police. Enraged, Franco declared martial law. Hundreds of Basques were arrested without warrants by the Guardia Civil, and many were tortured for information. Some were forced to stand up to their necks in ice water for hours.

Among those seized were priests suspected of helping ETA commandos. When the vicar general protested, he was told, "The priests had better watch their step. If they don't like it, we are preparing a reception center for them in Ifni" —a tiny arid Spanish enclave on the coast of Morocco.

The sixteen defendants were denied a civil trial, and were brought before a military court in Burgos. The prosecutor demanded death for six defendants, and a total of 728 years in jail for the other ten, including two priests and three women.

ETA commandos struck back in 1970 by kidnapping Eugen Beihl, the West German consul in the Basque provincial capital of San Sebastian. They warned that his fate would depend upon the outcome of the trial. Moderate ETA leaders criticized the abduction as a poor tactic, but staged a demonstration protesting the trial. In clashes with police a young worker was wounded by gunfire and died. Tension ran high as the court-martial opened.

After ETA defendant Mario Onaindia finished testifying, he plunged toward the dais where the five military judges sat and thundered his defiance at them: "Long live the Basque nation!"

His fifteen manacled co-defendants, including the two priests and three women, began struggling with their guards.

Seized, Onaindia refused to be subdued. One judge drew his saber and a guard aimed his pistol.

"Not here, you fool!" yelled another guard.

All the defendants, joined by their relatives present in the courtroom, burst out singing the forbidden Basque national anthem. The colonel in charge of the court-martial shouted for the chamber to be cleared. Spectators and newsmen were shoved roughly outside by the armed guards.

The court-martial proceeded in closed session. No argument was permitted in favor of the defendants. Six of them were condemned to die; ten were sentenced to long jail terms.

The world press reacted with disgust, charging that the Basques were being persecuted not for killing two Spanish police officials but for their separatist struggle.

Tens of thousands of Basques went on strike, mounting protest demonstrations. In a Bilbao suburb one crowd surged through the streets chanting, "Murderers! Basques, avenge the dead!" Police opened fire, wounding six persons.

As one ETA commando was executed, he sang a Basque separatist anthem. Hundreds of Basques attended the memorial service. His mother cried out, "They killed my son without justice. I ask the Basque people to unite and continue to fight!"

In 1971 anti-Franco demonstrations erupted throughout Europe. Spanish embassies were burned by demonstrators in three capitals. Fifteen European governments recalled their ambassadors from Madrid. Pope Paul VI and many other world leaders denounced Franco. Calling Franco a bloody murderer, Sweden's Prime Minister Olaf Palme took to the streets of Stockholm to collect money for the Basque resistance.

Stung and greatly upset by this international condemnation, Franco quickly organized a demonstration of 100,000 of his own supporters in Madrid. They were given signs to carry, reading: *Europe Wants to Suck Our Blood* and *Arriba, Franco*. The aging dictator made a quavering speech blaming the international criticism against him on "Communist terrorists" and a "leftist Masonic conspiracy."

The ETA was quick to avenge Franco's executions. A land mine blew up three members of the Guardia Civil in a jeep near Bilbao. The paramilitary police killed a Basque bar owner in retaliation. The ETA struck back by opening fire on a police station. In the gun battle the police killed two of their own men, as well as a family of three driving past the station.

To obtain the release of the West German consul, Franco was forced to commute the death sentences of the six condemned ETA commandos. The consul was turned loose unharmed on Christmas Day. Franco then changed the sentence of five of the other defendants, including Onaindia, to death. As an act of "mercy," he directed that they be executed by firing squads instead of the traditional garotte, a barbaric iron collar that snapped the spinal cord with the twist of a screw.

In November 1971 ETA commandos kidnapped Lorenzo Zabala, an industrialist who refused a pay raise to underpaid Basque workers in one of his factories. He was released when he agreed to the pay raise.

In April 1972 the ETA attacked local headquarters of the Falangist labor syndicates, the government unions scorned by most Spanish workers. The commandos also began blowing up yacht clubs and casinos where the wealthy oligarchy of Spain met for business and pleasure.

An explosive charge was planted beneath the green of a Madrid golf course where Franco was scheduled to play. It was discovered by security agents just before Franco's party reached that hole. Police arrested Basque suspects.

In January 1973 ETA commandos kidnapped leading industrialist Felipe Huarte, in support of his striking workers. Huarte was ransomed for $800,000 and agreed to settle the strike on his workers' terms. Defenders of these tactics pointed out that in a country where labor unions were illegal, workers had no legal way to achieve their demands through genuine collective bargaining.

From 1969 to 1974, ETA extremists were responsible for six assassinations, three kidnappings and forty bank raids, which netted $14 million for the Basque cause. During 1973 they planned their most daring operation—a plan aimed at the capture of Franco's premier, Admiral Luís Carrero.

They originally planned to kidnap him as a hostage to exchange for over 100 Basque political prisoners. But then they decided to assassinate him instead, eliminating the man expected to run Spain for Prince Juan Carlos after Franco died. The assassination was timed as a warning to judges trying a priest and nine underground labor leaders for "illegal association."

In December 1973 the commandos dug a tunnel beneath Madrid's busy Calle Serrano, planting huge charges of dynamite. When Carrero drove over the spot in a chauffeured limousine, the plunger was pushed. The blast shook the nearby United States embassy, digging a crater over eight feet deep and thirty feet wide.

Carrero's assassination enraged Franco, who instantly canceled all Basque passports in the hope of preventing the terrorists from escaping to France. Failing to catch them, he replaced Carrero with the chief of the Guardia Civil, Carlos Arias Navarro.

The trial of the priest and labor unionists ended with jail sentences of up to twenty years. Basque political prisoners protested by going on a hunger strike. The ETA appealed for a show of solidarity by all Basque workers. In December 1974 a general strike began in the Basque provinces and spread until over 200,000 workers had walked off their jobs.

Franco quickly imposed martial law on the Basque country. All personal liberties were suspended. The Guardia Civil made over 2,000 random arrests, flinging suspects into prison and torturing 250 of them for information. One priest was beaten so badly that he was hospitalized with a ruptured spleen, torn colon, and collapsed kidney. Another Basque, thrown back in his cell looking like a cadaver, begged to be killed and put out of his misery. The use of torture and sodium pentothal, or "truth serum," broke some prisoners. They exposed some ETA commando cells, resulting in many additional arrests and tortures.

In October 1975 the Franco regime put five more ETA terrorists before a firing squad. Even Basques who deplored the terrorist tactics of ETA extremists now became sympathizers. "I once thought the ETA was a bunch of murderers," declared a Basque businessman in San Sebastian. "Now I think it is the police who are murderers. I can't help preferring Basque killers to Spanish killers."

"No one is neutral anymore," said a Basque lawyer in Bilbao. "Franco has polarized everyone here. You're either pro-ETA or pro-Franco, and there aren't many of the latter."

The government unofficially organized pro-Franco elements into a paramilitary force called the *Guerrilleros de Cristo Rey* ("Warriors of Christ the King"). These street thugs brutally beat up Basque priests and lawyers, and bombed Basque bookshops and other suspected ETA hangouts.

Forcing their way into the home of a mother of one of the executed ETA prisoners, the *guerrilleros* savagely pistol-whipped her and her two children. Spanish police ignored the assault.

Juan Etxabe, an ETA exile in France who had once hung by his thumbs for twelve hours in a Spanish jail, said, "The *guerrilleros* killed my brother in Spain, they planted a bomb in my car here, and blew up my elder brother's restaurant in Bayonne. But they won't stop us. . . . It doesn't matter how many of our militants they murder. We are never at a loss for replacements because Madrid is fighting the entire Basque people, not just ETA. If it wasn't for the support of the Basques, ETA would long ago have ceased to exist."

An estimated 30 percent of the Basque people risked their freedom and lives for the ETA by providing hideouts, food, money, and medical aid for wounded commandos. Others kept silent when questioned by the Guardia Civil. Village priests often hid ETA militants from the police. Over 80 percent of Basque priests were believed to be involved with the ETA independence movement.

"We Basques are a suppressed minority fighting for our national identity," said Father Pierre Larzabal, head of a

Basque refugee organization in France. "Christ used violent means to expel the merchants from the Temple, and Joan of Arc, France's patron saint, led an army against the English. Our struggle is to expel the Spanish Fascist police who have invaded the Basque homeland."

He added, "ETA has been accused by the Franco government of being Communist, but that isn't so. They believe there is a God. They are a liberation movement without a doctrine, Socialists without a model." The Basques, he said, needed to cooperate with all anti-Francoists—ETA, Communists, Socialists, and moderates—to end Francoism and win liberation.

The illegal Basque National Party continued to eschew violence, concentrating instead on keeping the Basque culture—language, dances, and other customs—alive despite Franco's prohibitions. PNV leaders were jailed for violating these laws, for conducting anti-Spanish boycotts, and for spreading pro-independence propaganda.

While disapproving of ETA violence, the PNV nevertheless cooperated with the ETA in helping commando fugitives escape over the border to France.

By 1975 over half the top leadership of the ETA had been jailed, killed in shootouts with police, or executed. In October 1975 Franco announced that fifteen more Basque political prisoners would be brought to trial and, if found guilty, executed.

ETA commandos in France vowed to avenge the executions by assassinating political leaders of the Franco regime. A San Sebastian businessman who supported the ETA declared, "If more Basques are executed there will be bad trouble up here. We Basques will play mongoose to the Fascist cobra in Madrid."

There was great rejoicing among Basques when Franco died in November 1975. Juan Carlos was proclaimed king of Spain. The Basques lost no time in escalating their drive for a Basque republic.

In the northern Basque province of Álava, 5,000 workers went out on strike in March 1976. Meeting illegally in churches of the capital, Vitoria, they demanded higher wages and local self-government. Police ordered them to disperse. When they refused, riot squads flung tear gas bombs into the churches, opening fire with machine guns as gasping Basques fled. Over 100 workers were wounded, and 3 killed.

Infuriated, huge crowds of Basques poured into the district. Erecting barricades, they fought the police. Local Basque officials declared themselves "profoundly disgusted by the government's acts." Over 30,000 Basques gathered at the cathedral for the slain workers' funeral. Workers in Bilbao, Pamplona, and other Basque cities shut down hundreds of factories in sympathy.

The following month Franco's hard-line prime minister, Carlos Arias Navarro, cracked down on the "troublemakers." Another eighty-seven Basque activists were seized and flung in jail.

Two days after Juan Carlos I was sworn in as king, an ETA commando squad killed the mayor of a small Basque town known to be an informer for the Guardia Civil.

Juan Carlos sought to allay widespread impatience for reform of the brutal Franco regime. He proclaimed a partial amnesty for political prisoners. But he released only one of seven Basque priests imprisoned in the Concordat jail at Zamora under a combined sentence of 102 years. Even that priest was immediately rearrested and returned to the jail.

The ETA announced that it would continue its fight for Basque independence. "We know that no Spanish king is going to meet our demands," declared one commando. "The changeover in power in Madrid means nothing to us. Our struggle continues as before." Another said, "History has shown us that true changes are accomplished through revolutionary means. The future belongs to the rifle."

But Spain was moving toward change. In elections held in 1977—even with the election machinery still in the hands of the Francoist bureaucracy—almost 55 percent of the vote favored leftist parties. The voters demanded a quick end to Francoism and speedy restoration of full democracy.

In September 30,000 Basques demonstrated in Pamplona demanding total amnesty, legalization of all political parties, and autonomy for the Basque region. Marching behind Basque flags of red, white, and green, they shouted for the dismissal of all Francoist ministers from the government.

Basque veterans of the Spanish Civil War held their first legal meeting under the sacred oak tree of Guernica, symbol of the free spirit of the Basques. They then attended a requiem mass near Guernica in memory of their fallen comrades.

In 1977 the Madrid government finally agreed to negotiate with Basque nationalist leaders on a self-rule statute for the Basque country. A series of royal decrees opened the door for the reestablishment of autonomous governments for the Basques, as well as for the fiercely independent Catalans of Barcelona.

In October King Juan Carlos and his government pressed New York City's Museum of Modern Art, where Picasso's famous mural *Guernica* had hung since 1939, to return it to Spain. Picasso's will had specified that the painting be given to Spain after the rise of a truly democratic Spanish republic.

Basques insisted that the mural must hang in a Guernica museum. The New York museum authorities promised to return the priceless mural eventually, when it could be assured of protection against Fascist vandalism. Art critics agreed that the mural, like the Basque passion for freedom, would continue to evoke world admiration long after the Spanish dictator who hated both was forgotten.

Meanwhile the ETA, uncompromising in its demand for total separation from Spain and independence, continued its unrelenting pressure through terrorism. Its leaders were convinced that by murdering enough Spanish police and creating the appearance of anarchy, they could make Spain's new democratic government look fatally weak.

They hoped to provoke the Spanish army, still molded in the image of Franco Fascism, to overthrow the government in the name of preserving Spanish unity. This would bring a reign of right-wing terror to the Basque provinces, driving even the most moderate Basques into the arms of the ETA. With total Basque unity, ETA leaders reasoned, they could fight a guerrilla war of secession to final victory.

In March 1978 a group of ETA guerrillas with machine guns and hand grenades attacked a nuclear power plant in the Basque region. In July of that same year, during the annual "running of the bulls" festival in Pamplona, the ETA mounted a pro-Basque demonstration which was broken up by Spanish riot police in a ten-hour battle. The fighting spread to San Sebastian, the Basque capital, where the ETA threw up street barricades, and in Bilbao, where buses and shops were set afire in a four-hour pitched battle.

"We appear to be living on a powder magazine that may go off at any time," said a San Sebastian shopkeeper.

In an effort to pacify the Basques, the alarmed Madrid government quickly replaced the governors of three Basque provinces, and transferred several police chiefs to other parts of Spain. It also recognized the Basques' right to use their own language and display their national flag. These concessions infuriated Francoists in the Spanish police and military.

The ETA began murdering Spanish police in the Basque country at the rate of one a day. In Bilbao 800 enraged police mutinied and rioted against the Madrid government, shouting slogans like "The Army to Power!"

Basque moderates, who were willing to settle for Basque autonomy under the Spanish flag, clashed with the ETA separatists in October 1978. Both factions staged marches in Bilbao on the same day, and police fired tear gas and rubber bullets to break up the ETA supporters.

When ETA terrorists killed a judge who had sentenced many Basque separatists to prison, national police engaged ETA suspects in a gun battle. Firing indiscriminately into a crowded plaza, the police killed a housewife and three other civilian bystanders. Leftist Basque parties and unions called a strike in San Sebastian in protest.

In December 1978, as the Madrid government prepared for elections designed to officially turn the country into a parliamentary democracy, the ETA went into action to boycott and discredit the elections. Two members of the parliamentary civil guard were killed by a land mine in the Basque region and there were twenty-five such murders during October and November.

The Tuesday before the election, the ETA assassinated three more policemen. At midnight before election day, ETA guerrillas seized the television station in San Sebastian and urged a boycott of the polls because the new constitution would grant only limited autonomy to the Basque region. In the whole Basque region only a few dozen voters showed up to cast ballots. But the sixty percent of Spain's eligible voters who did vote approved the constitution.

In January 1979, ETA gunmen assassinated a Spanish Supreme Court judge, an army major, and two policemen. Three masked ETA guerrillas broke into the San Sebastian public library and ripped the Spanish flag off its flagpole, while Basque separatists cheered in the street. Riot police fired rubber bullets and smoke grenades to disperse the demonstrators, who hurled rocks at the police.

Spanish rightists demanded that the Madrid government take military action against the Basque region. "We could go in and seal off the borders and have it all cleaned up within a month and a half," an army colonel insisted. One group of civil guards, police, and army officers was found to be plotting to overthrow the Madrid government for its "timidity" in dealing with the Basques.

In July 1979 the ETA waged war on Spain's lucrative tourist trade by planting fifteen time bombs in favorite vacation spots along the southern coast, and warning tourists away. The Paris-to-Madrid express was also attacked by machine gun fire after France stopped providing political sanctuary to Basque rebels. Restaurants in many Basque towns carried signs stating: *We do not serve Frenchmen.*

In October the Basque provinces were finally permitted to vote on home rule. The election was boycotted by the ETA, which claimed it was an attempt to weaken the independence movement. But 88 percent of Basques who did vote favored a plan giving the Basques control over their own language, culture, education, taxes, local government, and police but still keeping them under the thumb of the hated national police.

The ETA threatened to continue its guerrilla warfare until

the Basque regions won their independence as a nation. And right-wing army circles, furious at the home rule concessions to the Basques, threatened a coup to restore the old Franco policies.

The Madrid government, besieged on one hand by ETA terrorism and on the other by the threat of a Fascist resurgence, is hopeful that home rule will succeed in ending the problem. But it seems unlikely that there will be peace in Spain until decrees are signed that fully restore the Basques' ancient rights.

10

"FIDEL! FIDEL! FIDEL!"

The Cuban Revolt Against Tyranny

Polls of voters in Cuba revealed to presidential candidate General Fulgencio Batista that he would get fewer votes than anyone else in the scheduled elections. Before sunrise on March 10, 1952, he led a group of his military supporters into Camp Columbia. Seizing and arresting the Cuban army commanders, he proclaimed himself the new chief of state of Cuba.

American corporations were pleased. They knew Batista could be bribed to grant them lucrative privileges in Cuba. His regime was promptly recognized by the United States.

The dictator suspended Cuba's twelve-year-old constitution. Dissolving all political parties, he decreed that all legislative and executive powers would flow from him. He nullified all laws that displeased him, especially those providing for land reform. Civil liberties were set aside. Radio stations were placed under government control. The Cuban press was forbidden to publish anything critical of the Batista regime.

The first Cubans to protest the loss of their liberties were university students. They staged four-day mock funeral cere-

monies for the Cuban constitution, which they literally buried in a coffin. They would attend no more classes, they announced, until democracy was restored. Batista ordered
troops to attack the students, who were beaten, shot, and
killed.

Cubans who protested were arrested and tortured.

One frustrated candidate for the Cuban Congress in the
blocked elections, a young lawyer, wrote an indignant letter
to Batista. He predicted that the dictator's regime would be
marked by graft, corruption, torture, and murder, and would
eventually be overthrown by the enraged Cuban people. The
writer of the letter signed himself Fidel Castro.

Nine days later Castro petitioned Cuba's Supreme Court
to declare the Batista regime unconstitutional, and to sentence the dictator to 100 years in prison. But the court,
which feared Batista's power, ruled that "revolution is the
source of law." If that was the case, Castro decided, then the
only hope of restoring human rights in Cuba was another
revolution.

Batista lost no time in making lucrative deals with American-owned companies. Utilities were allowed to raise their
rates for gas and electricity. Sugar growers, mining companies, and oil refineries were granted substantial tax reduc-
tions. Taking graft from a building boom in Havana, Batista
pocketed one out of every five dollars spent in construction.

In six years the "gratitude" of the big corporations would
be reflected in Batista's personal fortune, estimated in 1958
at more than $500 million. The boom in Havana impressed
American tourists and businessmen, but did not touch the
lives of two-thirds of the Cubans living in rural poverty.

Mounting opposition to his regime forced Batista to shut
down newspapers and jail editors. Secret police wielding

submachine guns arrested political opponents, carting them off to be tortured in police stations. One morning ninety-two corpses were heaped at a Havana street intersection as a warning to dissenters. Many politicians fled to Miami.

Castro and a group of his friends met secretly to plot revolution. Pooling their savings, they purchased weapons and ammunition for an attack on Fort Moncada in Santiago de Cuba. They hoped to spark a popular revolt that would topple the dictator and restore democracy to Cuba.

July 26, 1953, the target date, was carnival night in Santiago de Cuba. People caroused in the streets, and security at the fort was relaxed. Leading 170 university students, Castro surprised the sentries, but they were then quickly surrounded by troops and raked with machine-gun fire.

Ten students were killed, and most of the rest were captured and tortured. Sixty were slain in prison.

Other prisoners were tried in secret. On October 16, 1953, Castro made an impassioned speech, declaring, "We have been raised listening to talk of liberty, justice and rights. . . . The island will first sink into the sea before we will consent to be the slaves of anyone! . . . Condemn me—it doesn't matter. History will absolve me!"

He and the others were convicted and sentenced to fifteen years imprisonment on the Isle of Pines. Refusing to be silenced, Castro smuggled revolutionary messages and articles out of jail for clandestine publication. He was punished for this by solitary confinement on bread and water.

But his agitation met with an eager response from the youth of Cuba. The Twenty-sixth of July Movement was formed, named after the day that Castro's group attacked Moncada.

Prodded by the United States, Batista arranged elections

in November 1954 to legitimize his rule. But the only other candidate withdrew, charging that the elections were rigged. Batista held them anyhow, and won "unopposed."

The dictator sent Castro word that he was willing to grant amnesty and exile to all political prisoners if Castro would agree to dissolve the Twenty-sixth of July Movement. Castro scornfully refused. Batista declared an amnesty anyhow, when his advisers suggested that it would be safer to kick the jailed revolutionaries out of the country than to keep them in Cuba as martyr symbols for the Twenty-sixth of July Movement.

Prisoners released from the Isle of Pines were cheered by crowds of flag-waving supporters en route to a deportation center. A delegation of women in black, mothers in mourning for sons lost in the Moncada raid, sang Cuba's national anthem. The Twenty-sixth of July rebels shouted, "Liberty or death!" as they were loaded on a ship that would carry them to exile in Mexico.

In 1955 the exiles organized and trained in Mexico City for a revolutionary invasion of Cuba. The island's leading intellectuals sent Castro assurances of their support, and helped raise funds for the Twenty-sixth of July Movement. Poor people in Cuban villages contributed precious pesos and centavos to the cause symbolized by Castro. Money also came from American sympathizers.

"I handled nearly twenty thousand pesos," Castro recalled later. "Yet how many times we were lacking milk for my son! How many times did the hardhearted electric company cut off my electricity! I still keep the miserable court papers by which the landowners dispossess tenants. I had no personal income, but practically lived on the charity of my friends. I know what it is like to see a son suffering from hunger while having, in my pockets, money belonging to the cause."

In Mexico City, Castro was joined by revolutionist Ernesto ("Che") Guevara, who had fled after the fall of the leftist government in Guatemala. Guevara and Fidel's brother Raúl became chief lieutenants for the Twenty-sixth of July Movement.

Batista, meanwhile, continued to grow wealthier by stealing from the Cuban treasury and taking graft from American corporations. United States Ambassador Earl E. T. Smith, a defender of United States business interests and no friend of Castro's, admitted later that "the corruption of the Batista government had sickened the Cuban people. They wanted a change."

Batista's secret police beat up newspapermen suspected of making anti-Batista allusions in their writings. Police also broke into homes at midnight to arrest and torture suspected opponents of the regime, who were never seen again.

Batista knew that the poor of Cuba were secretly supporting the Twenty-sixth of July Movement. To terrorize them he had defenseless peasants lashed with machetes, and laborers beaten with rifle butts. Faces were scarred, ribs and bones broken. Any who tried to seek legal redress in the courts for these assaults were thrown in jail or murdered.

In 1956 Castro and his followers prepared to invade Cuba. He set a date for his underground supporters on the island to stage simultaneous uprisings. But a storm delayed the battered old sailing vessel that brought Castro, Guevara and eighty-two other exiles back to Cuba. As their ship reached the western coast of Oriente Province on December 2, they learned by radio that the uprisings had already taken place.

Desperate fighting had caused Batista to declare martial law in four provinces. Military reinforcements had been rushed to Oriente. The revolt had been crushed, and most of the revolutionists had been killed or captured.

"We shall still win," Fidel Castro comforted his downcast followers, "because the people are still with us."

Discovered as they splashed ashore, Castro and his company were bombed and strafed as they fled to the concealment of nearby sugarcane fields. A Radio Havana bulletin claimed that Castro and forty-two followers had been killed on the beachhead.

A thousand government troops roamed the countryside searching for them. There were sporadic gun duels. Many of the starved, exhausted expeditionaries could scarcely move, let alone fight. Some sought refuge in peasant huts where Batista's soldiers lay in hiding. They were quickly killed.

Castro led a small group of survivors on night marches toward the Sierra Maestra. By day they hid in sugarcane fields, jungles, and mangrove swamps to escape the planes that were searching for them. By night they were concealed and fed by local peasants. Castro insisted upon paying for everything. "We are not robbers like Batista's soldiers," he declared.

Only a dozen revolutionaries reached the shelter of the mountains. With their feet bleeding, and tongues swollen from thirst after four days under the burning sun, each man had less than ten cartridges left for his rifle. They made their camp in an 8,000-foot-high hideout at Pico Turquino.

A group of campesinos ("peasants") asked Castro if he would correct an injustice they had suffered. Their small farms had been confiscated by the foreman of an absentee landowner. The foreman had accused them of being rebel sympathizers.

Castro and his men seized the foreman. A "revolutionary trial" was held in the mountains with Raúl Castro, Che Guevara, and Fidel as judges. After the campesinos testified, the revolutionary court found the foreman guilty. He was executed, and the farms he had seized were returned to their owners. Word spread like wildfire through Oriente Province. Justice for the poor had returned to Cuba with the leaders of the Twenty-sixth of July Movement!

In January 1957 Batista covered the province with posters offering a secret reward of up to $100,000 for "the head of Fidel Castro." But a close bond of cooperation was forged swiftly between the people of Oriente and the rebel leader, who became the focus of Cuban hopes for the future.

Castro organized open-air schools and clinics in the forest.

The *campesinos* shared what little they had with his band, and served as messengers, spies, and saboteurs. They brought Castro stolen arms, and arranged to print and circulate his leaflets. He carefully kept every promise he made to them, and won their affection as well by always treating them with respect.

Because shaving was a nuisance and amenities few, Castro and his men grew beards. As the *barbudos* ("bearded ones") they soon became heroes among the rural and urban poor of Cuba, as well as among the island's students. Many young peasants joined Castro's forces.

Fidel, Che Guevara, and Raúl Castro led raids on government strongholds in nearby towns. They were aided by workers who paralyzed the Batista forces by sabotaging public transport, electric power, and communications.

Infuriated, Batista launched a new campaign of terror to crush popular support for the Twenty-sixth of July Movement. Almost half the barefoot *campesinos* of Oriente Province, including women and children, were forced out of their villages and into the cities. Batista's air force then bombed their huts with napalm, depriving Castro of the aid of those villages.

Every sunrise revealed dozens of corpses of suspected Castro sympathizers hanging from lamp posts or lying crumpled on the pavement. Two accused men were decapitated, their heads exhibited to the people from a cruising jeep. In Santiago a fifteen-year-old boy was tortured for twenty-four hours, then killed by driving nails into his forehead.

Revulsion was so widespread that even one of Batista's intimate friends begged him to stop the atrocities. Batista finally permitted the *campesinos* of Oriente to return home, but his planes continued to bomb suspected villages. Foreign correspondents were not permitted to write about these events. They were fed government propaganda, including the fabrication that the dead bodies of Fidel and Raúl Castro had been found.

In November 1956 the Twenty-sixth of July Movement issued a widely circulated call to arms to all the people of Cuba. All groups that had vainly sought to get rid of Batista through elections were urged to join a revolution for social justice.

"By social justice," the manifesto declared, "the 26th of July Movement understands the establishment of an order such that all inalienable rights of the human person—political, social, economic and cultural—are fully satisfied and guaranteed. . . . Because we were deprived of those very rights, we have been fighting since the tenth of March, 1952."

Castro promised immediate freedom for all political and military prisoners; free speech and full civil rights for everyone; and elections one year after Batista's overthrow. He called upon the United States to stop supplying Batista with the arms used to kill Cuban workers, peasants, and students.

The manifesto of November 1956 united every social class and occupational group behind the Twenty-sixth of July Movement. Professors, priests, lawyers, doctors, tradesmen, carpenters, refinery workers, fishermen, and peasants joined the resistance movement. Some enlisted in Castro's guerrilla forces in the Sierra Maestra; most organized secretly at home.

The Communist party, ironically, held back because of its uneasy truce with the Batista regime. The Communists refused to commit themselves to the Twenty-sixth of July Movement until events showed that it was going to succeed. In February 1957 the Communists expressed "radical disagreement with the tactics and plans" of Castro. They condemned his use of sabotage, the burning of sugarcane fields, and counter-terror against Batista's forces.

On July 30, 1957, Oriente rebel leader Frank País was discovered hiding in the home of a prominent businessman in Santiago de Cuba. He and his protector were shot by Police Chief Colonel José Salas Cañizares. The next day United States Ambassador Earl T. Smith visited Santiago's mayor to receive the keys to the city during a diplomatic visit. He was embarrassed when the women of Santiago, dressed in mourning, used the occasion to stage a protest in the town plaza. They carried a banner reading: *Stop Killing Our Sons! The Mothers of Cuba.* Singing the Cuban national anthem, they shouted, "Liberty! Liberty!"

Firemen turned high-pressure hoses on them, sweeping some off their feet. The police chief shoved others away roughly, ordering them to disperse. When they refused, police beat them with clubs and flung some into a police wagon.

Pressed for a statement by foreign newsmen, Ambassador Smith said, "I think it unfortunate that some of the people of Santiago de Cuba took advantage of my presence here to demonstrate and protest to their own government."

When Smith realized how callous his statement made the

United States seem, he later gave reporters an amended reaction: "Any form of excessive police action is abhorrent to me."

All of Santiago shut down for the funerals of the two murdered men. The shutdown turned into a general strike, which spread to other cities. Batista again suspended all civil rights, imposing total censorship. Homes were searched without warrant. Cubans were arrested and held without trial.

A revolutionary group of students attempted to capture the presidential palace and failed. Over forty were killed.

In the fall of 1957 a navy mutiny broke out in the port of Cienfuegos. Joined by the townspeople, the mutineers ran up the banner of the Twenty-sixth of July Movement. Batista swiftly dispatched army planes to bomb the city. Much of the population was wiped out, along with the rebellion. Army bulldozers pushed hundreds of bodies into open ditches in a mass burial.

In November 1957 Castro and his men attacked the city of Manzanillo. Holding it for several hours, he stripped the garrison of weapons and captured 150 soldiers. To their astonishment, he simply reproached them for fighting for a dictator against the people, then let them go. The rebels observed humane rules, Castro explained, and did not execute or harm military prisoners who had not committed atrocities.

In that same month the Pentagon indicated its support of Batista. United States Air Force Major General Truman Landon was sent to Havana to bestow the Legion of Merit on the head of Batista's air force, Colonel Carlos Tabernilla, who had directed the air attack on the population of Cienfuegos. United States Marine Corps General Lemuel C. Shepherd assured Batista that Washington considered him "a great president." These tributes were played up in the Batista press to impress Cubans with American support for the dictator.

The Cuban people continued their struggle for liberation, using homemade bombs to blow up trucks, trains, bridges, public buildings, and the homes of Batista officials. Batista retaliated by hanging suspects from trees and lamp posts. Many were shot in cars, with grenades planted on them to justify the murders. One fifty-year-old teacher, a mother of three children, was dragged out of bed at midnight and tortured in a police station until dawn for information she did not have.

"The thing that made the people hate Batista was very simple," said a shoe salesman turned rebel. "He killed too many of them. He just killed too many people."

News of the atrocities was censored in the Batista press, but traveled swiftly by word of mouth. One upset Havana magistrate denounced Batista's uniformed murderers openly in court. The dictator retaliated by suspending all civilian court trials.

In February 1958 Castro issued the first decree of the Twenty-sixth of July Movement. Summary courts-martial were authorized for counterrevolutionary murder, torture, arson, and looting. Penalties included execution by firing squad. The decree was intended to give pause to Batista's criminals in uniform.

By now the Twenty-sixth of July Movement involved almost all the people of Cuba. Workers, whose unions were held captive by Batista officials, cooperated with outraged small business owners, doctors, lawyers, teachers, clerks, and clergy. All saw Fidel Castro as their only hope to rid themselves of a tyrant.

Batista was dismayed when the hierarchy of the Cuban Catholic church met in Havana to "suggest" that his resignation would avoid further bloodshed. Dr. José Miró Cardona, head of the Cuban Bar Association, demanded that the dictator step aside for a new provisional government. Batista immediately ordered his arrest. Hiding Miró Cardona, the Church helped smuggle him out of Cuba disguised as a priest.

Popular defiance grew. Demands for Batista's resignation came from such Cuban organizations as the Masons, Lions, Catholic Action, and associations of doctors, dentists, engineers, accountants, and journalists.

The United States Central Intelligence Agency warned the Eisenhower administration that continued support for Batista would boomerang badly if the dictator fell. Ambassador Smith was ordered to pressure Batista to restore civil rights and permit honest elections. The dictator reluctantly agreed, and set new elections for June 1, 1958. But he excluded Oriente Province from any restoration of human rights or participation in the elections.

When high school students in Santiago demonstrated in protest, police attacked and killed several of them. Students in Pinar del Río marched to protest this latest atrocity, and were also shot down. Infuriated students and parents all over Cuba called a nationwide school strike.

In shortwave radio broadcasts from the Sierra Maestra, Castro called upon the Cuban people to rise and wage "total war" on the Batista regime. Government supply trucks, trains, and warehouses began going up in flames.

Batista reimposed full censorship and martial law, canceling the elections. This repudiation of his promise to Washington left the State Department no choice. All United States military aid to the Cuban dictatorship was now embargoed.

"Cubans, freedom depends on you!" Castro cried in a shortwave broadcast. "Let us show America and the world that Cubans know how to depose tyrannies by a general strike. Liberty or death!" Workers responded by calling the general strike.

This tactic failed because the Communist party, the most powerful faction in the Cuban Federation of Labor, promised to support the strike, then failed to do so. The Communist defection caused the slaughter of the workers who had exposed themselves by striking; Batista's police quickly rounded them up and murdered many in prison, as they would not have dared to do had the whole Cuban labor force brought the Cuban economy to a standstill.

In May 1958 Batista made an all-out effort to wipe out the rebel forces in the Sierra Maestra. A massive army offensive was backed by the air force. The government forces outnumbered Castro's guerrillas in the mountains by over thirty to one. "But their forces were spread out searching for us," Castro recalled later, "and we could choose the most favorable conditions to fight."

Castro's men mined the approaches to their camp and set up concealed machine-gun posts. Only 1,000 of Batista's soldiers reached the inner ring of mines, and not a single soldier was able to penetrate it. Hundreds were captured, indoctrinated, then released. Batista's offensive failed.

Castro then signaled for a counterattack. Sweeping out of the Sierra Maestra, he and his men destroyed railroad bridges, blocked roads, burned government trucks, and shut down electric plants and oil refineries. Batista's forces blockaded Oriente Province, and food became scarce. Guerrillas and civilians had to subsist for days on raw sugarcane.

The people did not complain. "Should we not support our

own sons who are fighting for us?" asked one old man. The *campesinos* served as Castro's eyes and ears. He knew at once when, where, and in what strength any Batista unit moved.

Rebels in Havana struck at night at Batista's police and troops known to have tortured suspects. Twenty Batistianos were waylaid and killed, their bodies left in the streets.

On July 20, 1958, Cuba's middle-class professional societies entered into a formal alliance with Castro's Civil Revolutionary Front. Their pact agreed upon a "return to democracy" after Batista was overthrown.

As Castro's forces fought their way west, they were joined by swarms of volunteers. The rebels used loudspeakers to appeal to Batista's soldiers to desert, promising generous treatment. One army commander, who had been Castro's classmate at law school, was appealed to in the name of Cuban idealism. Surrendering his whole regiment and their arms, he and his men were allowed to join the rebels or go free.

News of Castro's generosity spread through Batista's forces. Soldiers and officers began to desert to the rebels in increasing numbers. As it became clear to Washington that Batista's days of power were ending, United States Ambassador Smith was ordered to work behind the scenes in Havana to thwart the succession of Castro. Smith sought to transfer power from Batista to a conservative military junta that could be depended upon to protect United States investments in Cuba. Castro's spies told him what was going on.

"If the U.S. Department of State," he warned Washington, "continues to become involved in the intrigues of Mr. Smith and Batista . . . we will know how to defend ourselves!"

Aware that time was rapidly running out for him, Batista sought to retain American support by announcing new presidential elections in which he would not run. On November 3,

1958, he held rigged elections, boycotted by most Cubans, in which a Batista puppet "won." It was clear that Batista intended to continue to wield the real power in Cuba.

"Batista's failure to live up to his solemn promise to me," said Ambassador Smith, "that he would hold free and open elections acceptable to the people was his last big mistake. . . . As a result of the elections he lost whatever followers he had left. The people were now completely disillusioned."

Four days after the fraudulent election, Castro began a full-scale offensive to bring down the dictatorship. One after another, towns and villages went over to him. Liberated Cubans everywhere greeted Castro with enthusiasm. As he drove west, Castro broadcast stirring appeals to all Cubans to rise with him and put their oppressors to flight.

By late December 1958 the ranks of the guerrillas had grown to 8,000. Supported by the whole countryside, they swept irresistibly across Cuba. Batista's troops either fled, surrendered, or joined the rebels. Santiago fell, then Santa Clara, the key city of central Cuba.

Batista knew he was finished. Then he learned that Ambassador Smith had conspired with one of Batista's top aides, General Eulogio Cantillo, to arrest him and seize power. Cantillo then planned to rule Cuba as head of a United States–supported military junta.

Batista decided not to wait for Cantillo's scheme or Castro's arrival in Havana. In the early hours of January 1, 1959, he fled Cuba by plane, and took refuge in the Dominican Republic, which was ruled by another dictator, Rafael Trujillo. Batista took $600 million from the Cuban treasury, money which he considered his private fortune. The island was left almost bankrupt.

News of the dictator's fall flashed throughout the country.

The pent-up fury against him and his henchmen exploded in an orgy of vengeful killing, especially in the provinces.

Castro broadcast an urgent radio appeal to the people not to take justice into their own hands. He promised that all Batistiano criminals would be arrested, tried, and punished under his February decree. Meanwhile, he urged, it was imperative for the revolution that order be preserved.

Ambassador Smith's plan failed. On January 8, 1959, Castro entered Havana in triumph. The streets were jammed with Cubans shouting themselves hoarse as they struggled for a glimpse of their deliverer. Bearded, grinning, and waving, Castro rode into the city astride a captured tank.

"Fidel! Fidel! Fidel!"

Shrugging off aides who tried to act as bodyguards, Castro plunged into the crowds shaking hands, walking from one end of the city to the other. He was safe among the people.

The Pentagon was baffled. How could a ragged little band of guerrilla fighters have whipped Batista's army of 50,000 American-trained regulars, equipped with tanks and planes? The explanation was that Batista's defeat had been less military than political. Batista had 50,000 troops, but Castro had nearly 6½ million Cubans.

"Revolutions, real revolutions do not arise through the will of one man or one group," Castro declared. "Revolutions are remedies—bitter remedies, yes. But at times revolution is the only remedy that can be applied to evils even more bitter."

A United States State Department white paper on Cuba issued more than two years later admitted, "The character of the Batista regime in Cuba made a violent popular reaction almost inevitable. The rapacity of the leadership, the corruption of the Government, the brutality of the police, the regime's indifference to the needs of the people for education, medical care, housing, for social justice and economic opportunity . . . constituted an open invitation to revolution."

Castro declared a three-day general holiday.

Cubans were delighted by their newly won freedom. The labor unions were freed from government control. The universities were open and free. Press censorship ended. Batista's police and spy apparatus were dismantled. Government graft ended. And elections were promised.

The archbishop of Santiago hailed Castro's victory as a "radical restoration" of the human rights denied by Batista.

Despite a bankrupt treasury, Castro moved swiftly to enact socialistic laws to aid the long-suffering masses, especially the landless peasants. A visiting professor from Notre Dame University, Samuel Shapiro, asked fishermen and farmers working in newly organized cooperatives whether they would like to do away with the Castro regime. "The response," he reported, "was always an astonished stare, laughter, or an outburst of anger."

Trusting Castro to do justice, the Cuban people did not take vengeance against the Batistianos. There was not a single lynching. Trials of "war criminals" for torture, murder, and rape were held in a Havana public square, attended by enormous crowds, and broadcast on TV. Witnesses testified, and those found guilty received severe sentences. Similar trials were held all over Cuba.

A storm of criticism erupted in the American press. Castro was denounced for initiating a "bloodbath." His regime was compared to that of the Jacobins in the French Reign of Terror. But even the conservative Catholic Church of Cuba defended the trials of the Batista criminals as "Operation Truth."

Castro asked his critics, "Would you have preferred the defendants to be mobbed and lynched, as collaborators and

Fascists were after France and Italy were liberated in World War II? Our public trials prevented that!"

He would visit as many as fifteen tiny villages in remote provinces in an exhausting twelve-hour day. *Guajiros* and their families would gather around Castro's jeep to give him firsthand information about their problems. "If I lost everyday contact with the people, with reality," Castro said, "I would feel very bad."

He listened thoughtfully to all complaints about the lack of public services and amenities. Making notes, he promised to correct justified grievances quickly, and did so. Coming across local baseball games, he would take off his shirt and play. He would chat and joke with children and old people, and often took coffee in the peasants' houses.

At harvest time Castro encouraged city volunteers to help bring in the sugarcane crop. He set an example himself by spending two weeks with the harvesters slashing and stacking cane alongside them. The poor of Cuba idolized Castro, affectionately calling him "Fidel."

But he became less popular with the Cuban middle classes, because he favored the poor at their expense. And they were disillusioned when he broke his promise to permit free elections, free speech, and a free press. These risks could not be taken, Castro explained, until after the revolution had established agrarian reforms, jobs for all, literacy for everyone, free public schools, and free hospitals.

"It is necessary to put an end to poverty, to consolidate the work of the revolution, before holding elections," he said.

The middle classes were stunned. Their cooperation with Castro had been based on his pledge to restore democracy. They now suspected that he had gone over to the Communists, committing himself to a class struggle of poor against well-to-do.

Thousands began leaving Cuba for exile in the United States. Their defection led the CIA to hatch a plot with Cuban refugees in Miami to overthrow and assassinate Castro. This conspiracy ended in the disastrous Bay of Pigs invasion.

Castro cited this unsuccessful attempt to overthrow him as justification for his refusal to give Cubans a bill of rights. He argued that such freedoms would only be used by the counterrevolutionaries, backed by the American CIA, to subvert and destroy Cuba's revolutionary government.

Most visitors to Cuba agree that the Cuban masses today are better off and happier than they were under the tyranny of Batista. They have the Soviet version of human rights—the right to a job, to a low-cost dwelling, to free medical care. But they are denied the democratic version of human rights—free elections, free speech, and a free press.

Under Castro, the only rights Cubans enjoy are those he chooses to grant them, according to the principle that now amounts to national law in Cuba: "Fidel knows best."

11

WHEN DEMOCRACY DIED IN INDIA

The Struggle to Overthrow Mrs. Gandhi's Dictatorship

"In India," Prime Minister Indira Gandhi told her people in 1975, "democracy was given too much license."

The previous year, a ruinous inflation had made it difficult for the workers of India to feed their families. In 1974 a million low-paid members of India's railway workers' union had gone out on strike, led by union head George Fernandes, who was also chairman of India's Socialist party. The strike plunged the country into a severe economic crisis. It was short-lived. Prime Minister Gandhi broke the strike by arresting Fernandes and thousands of union organizers.

Subsequently another Socialist, Raj Narain, accused Mrs. Gandhi of holding office illegally because she had violated India's election laws in winning her seat in Parliament. An Indian court upheld his charges, leading to calls for her resignation as prime minister. Instead she declared a state of emergency and assumed dictatorial powers.

Mass arrests of her opponents followed. One of those who escaped the dragnet by going underground was labor leader George Fernandes. From various hideouts he gave interviews to the international press. "It has been my constant appeal to the people . . . to get rid of this dictatorship," he declared.

For a whole year government police searched high and low for Fernandes. He embarrassed them by surfacing frequently at different places for new interviews, then vanishing before they could catch him. Fernandes claimed that he was being protected by supporters all over India.

On May 1, 1976, at 9:00 P.M., police entered the home of Fernandes's parents in Bangalore and seized his brother, Lawrence. He was interrogated in a police station until 3:00 A.M. as to the whereabouts of his brother George. When Lawrence swore that he didn't know, the police began torturing him.

He was beaten with a club until it broke. A second club was used until it also broke. The police went through five clubs, then whipped Fernandes with the root of a banyan tree. They also took turns kicking and punching him, and threatened to pitch him under a moving train. Finally he was imprisoned in solitary confinement, and starved for three days. On the fourth day he was found unconscious.

To conceal his identity, he was taken briefly to a hospital under a false name, then sent to another jail. His mother searched for him for three weeks before she finally located him in a prison cell. Emaciated from lack of food, he was paralyzed on the left side and his left hand and leg were swollen. Terror had left him with a stammer. He shook uncontrollably at the approach of anyone in uniform. He could not walk or even get up from the floor without the help of two people.

His mother appealed to the government for his release. She swore that neither Lawrence nor anyone else in the family knew where George was. Accusing police officials of torturing Lawrence, she begged for an investigation.

Soon afterward George Fernandes was arrested in Calcutta. His wife, who had gone to America, wrote to Mrs. Gandhi inquiring about her husband and protesting Lawrence's torture.

She received a reply from the Ministry of Home Affairs in New Delhi: "How can you not be aware of the activities of your husband, who has for the past several months been moving about instigating people to commit acts of violence, subversion, sabotage, and other serious crimes prejudicial to public order and the security of the country? He was arrested in Calcutta on 30th June and is in legal custody in connection with several criminal cases under investigation. He is in normal health." It added, "Allegation of torture of his brother Lawrence Fernandes is totally false, baseless, and mischievous."

George Fernandes's wife toured the United States and Europe publicizing the persecution of her husband and brother-in-law. What made the case significant was that it was not unusual. Tens of thousands of political opponents of Mrs. Gandhi were receiving the same treatment.

Indira Gandhi, daughter of the first prime minister of India, Jawaharlal Nehru, grew up accustomed to getting her own way. She was constantly encouraged to believe in her destiny as an elite leader of the Indian masses. "My favorite occupation," she recalled, "was to deliver thunderous speeches to the servants while standing on a high table."

Becoming prime minister in 1966, two years after her father's death, she was irked by the constraints of democracy in trying to deal with India's severe problems, particularly in the 1970s. Inflation ran out of control, food was scarce, electric power was short, the economy was stagnant, the treasury was empty. The corruption of her officials was so flagrant that riots broke out in protest. Police quelled the rioters, leaving ninety dead.

"There are visible signs," warned *Hindustan Times* editor B. G. Verghese, "of disintegration and enveloping chaos."

Mrs. Gandhi blamed India's troubles on its system of political democracy—copied from the United States, England, and France—calling it ill-suited to poor countries such as India. She claimed that reforms were blocked by constitutional guarantees of individual rights, elections, freedom of assembly, court appeals, and the rights of private property.

In June 1975 six minority parties put aside their differences to join together in the Janata (People's Front) party, to oppose Mrs. Gandhi in a by-election test of strength in the drought-ravaged state of Gujarat. Janata candidates ran for assembly seats held by Mrs. Gandhi's Congress party.

Mrs. Gandhi personally campaigned in broiling 110-degree weather, speaking at 120 meetings. The people of Gujarat were promised $20 million in drought relief funds and irrigation projects, plus special aid for the state's destitute untouchables—the lowest members of India's caste system whose touch or presence is regarded as polluting.

The day before the election, an Indian high court found Mrs. Gandhi guilty of Raj Narain's charges of corrupt election practices. She was dealt another crushing blow when the people of Gujarat went to the polls. Her Congress party lost 65 of the 140 state assembly seats it had previously held. The Janata won a majority of 87 seats.

Socialist Jaya Prakash Narayan, leader of the opposition in Parliament, demanded that Mrs. Gandhi resign. Addressing a huge rally in the walled city of Old Delhi, next to the modern capital, he warned that if she refused, a campaign of civil disobedience would be mounted to drive her out of office.

The crowd roared approval when Narayan called upon the

Indian army, police, and government to "protect democratic institutions" by ignoring Mrs. Gandhi's "illegal orders."

Morarji Desai, former deputy prime minister, explained to Italian correspondent Oriana Fallaci how a civil disobedience campaign would force Mrs. Gandhi's resignation.

"It consists of ignoring every prohibition, every law, every arrest, every police attack," he declared. "You stand there, the police charge into the crowd and beat you up and you don't react. You don't yield an inch. You don't need strength to do this, you don't need to eat. . . . She will be forced to go. Thousands of us will surround her house to prevent her going out or receiving visitors. We'll camp there night and day shouting to her to resign. Even if the police arrest us, beat us up, slaughter us. How many can they slaughter? And what will they do with the corpses? To prevent such action, Mrs. Gandhi has but one course open: to eliminate us all this very night."

Fallaci asked him, "What if . . . she decides to destroy you, the opposition?"

"All would be lost," he replied. "For us, for her, for the country. It would mean a dictatorship. And one day the lady would bitterly regret it."

When Mrs. Gandhi defied the court decision, a full week of protest marches, strikes, and picketing sought to force her to step down.

"The opposition has only one aim," she cried angrily, "and that is to remove me from power. They have no other program of their own to help the country!"

The president of the Congress party proclaimed, "India is Indira, and Indira is India." The *Hindustan Times* called this view that Mrs. Gandhi was indispensable "no less than a Fuehrer principle." An opposition member declared in Parliament, "As of the moment the court delivered its ruling,

India has been without a legal Prime Minister. It is up to India to decide how to deal with this imposter."

Mrs. Gandhi's woes were compounded by her loss of support from her own Congress party. Members of the left agreed with Narayan that the government and Congress party leadership were hopelessly corrupt. Members of the right wanted Mrs. Gandhi replaced by the minister of agriculture, Jagjivan Ram.

It seemed inconceivable to Mrs. Gandhi, and to her politically ambitious son Sanjay, that the daughter of Jawaharlal Nehru should be driven from office. Sanjay urged his mother to take all power into her own hands and teach her opponents "a lesson they'll never forget." Under the Indian constitution, the prime minister has the right to declare a national emergency, suspend civil liberties, and exercise unlimited powers for as long as the emergency lasts.

On June 26, 1975, Mrs. Gandhi proclaimed such a state of emergency. All laws were set aside, and her decrees became law. In a nationwide radio address she spoke of India's need of "firm action . . . an iron will and the strictest discipline." Billboards appeared proclaiming: EMERGENCY, AN ERA OF DISCIPLINE.

She staged a series of rallies to whip up public support. The emergency was defended as necessary to foil the "deep and widespread conspiracy of Nazi politicians" to oust her, creating "a threat to law and order." She insisted that "The steps we have taken are to strengthen our democracy," and she promised to end bureaucratic corruption, crippling strikes, and profiteering.

Police rounded up 1,100 of her leading political opponents and critics and threw them into jail. Overseas cable and telex lines were cut for several hours to block transmission of news reports. Strict censorship was imposed upon both the Indian press and foreign journalists. All anti-government demonstrations, meetings, and "shouting of slogans" were forbidden.

These moves threw many cities of India into an uproar. In Old Delhi hundreds of youths poured into the bazaar shouting, "Kill the police!" and "Indira Gandhi, get off your throne!" A few hurled stones. Riot police swinging lead-tipped canes smashed into their ranks. Thirty youths were jailed.

Other demonstrators surged through Calcutta, Bombay, and cities in Bihar. Police broke up the demonstrations by opening fire on the protesters, killing several.

Reporters who tried to report the disorders found their stories blacked out by censors stationed in Delhi and all the state capitals. One reporter asked angrily just what he could report to his readers. "Only good news," he was told. Journalists were instructed to dwell on the government's achievements, and forbidden to report "objectionable matter," including any attacks made in Parliament on Mrs. Gandhi.

When journalists and editors defied these efforts to handcuff the press, some were jailed and others fired. Five New Delhi newspapers were shut down. The press was not even permitted to reveal that censorship had been imposed.

Foreign correspondents who filed stories about what was going on had their papers and magazines banned in India. Mrs. Gandhi's government demanded that foreign journalists sign a pledge to submit to censorship. Those who refused were deported. Officials at airports kept a blacklist of journalists who were forbidden to enter the country.

"In ten years of covering the world from Franco's Spain to Mao's China," reported Newsweek's Loren Jenkins, "I have never encountered such stringent and all-encompassing censorship." The Ministry of Information and Broadcasting denied this charge, blandly insisting that in India the press's "freedom of operation has been singularly free from any type of interference." The government, the ministry explained, had merely "improved the quantity and quality" of the news.

Narayan, the Socialist leader in Parliament, urged continuation of the civil disobedience campaign. He challenged Mrs. Gandhi to honor him by jailing him, as her father and Mahatma Gandhi had been jailed in their struggle for freedom.

A fleet of police cars surrounded the Gandhi Peace Foundation, where Narayan worked. The ailing seventy-two-year-old dissident—whom Indians called *Loknayah* ("the People's Hero") because he distributed food to the starving without diverting funds to his own pocket—was seized and marched off to prison. "Those whom the gods would destroy," he sighed, "they first make mad."

From jail he wrote Mrs. Gandhi a letter that was circulated widely in the underground. "You are reported to have said that democracy is not more important than the nation," he declared. "It is a false choice that you have formulated. There is no choice between democracy and the nation."

On Mrs. Gandhi's orders, police fanned through Indian towns and villages in mass midnight raids. Tens of thousands of her political opponents and critics were arrested and imprisoned without trial. Many others went into hiding or fled the country.

Among those seized was the seventy-nine-year-old Morarji Desai, the former deputy prime minister. He was taken off to jail with yarn and a spinning wheel, in the manner of Mahatma Gandhi when arrested by the British in earlier times. Another prisoner was Raj Narain, the Socialist rival in Mrs. Gandhi's hometown of Allahabad who had accused her of illegal election methods.

More than 400 politicians in the anti-Gandhi state of Madhya Pradesh were also jailed. One estimate put the total number of people imprisoned and held without trial during the emergency at 100,000.

Formerly outspoken Indians now refused to talk on telephones, fearful that their lines were being bugged. At meetings and luncheons they whispered political comments, glancing nervously over their shoulders whenever a passerby or waiter drew near enough to hear what they were saying.

Despite Mrs. Gandhi's attempts to censor people's knowledge of what she was doing, enough details got through the outside world to create international shock. Protests poured in from many countries.

Seeking to silence their criticism, Mrs. Gandhi assembled a purged and fearful Parliament in August 1975 to ratify her state of emergency and decrees. Entry into the Parliament was guarded by police, who checked visitors' passes as often as five times. Journalists were forbidden to publish anything about the session except the statements of government ministers.

"The very summoning of Parliament," Mrs. Gandhi declared, "has proved that democracy is functioning in India." Her brand of democracy functioned so well that Parliament voted her the power to postpone national elections indefinitely—at least until she could be sure of winning one.

The truncated Parliament also passed new laws to make Mrs. Gandhi's power absolute. The illegal election acts of which she had been convicted were made retroactively legal. The Supreme Court was denied the right to declare any of Mrs. Gandhi's decrees unconstitutional. All political prisoners were denied the right to appeal their imprisonment.

One disillusioned Congress party member denounced

these measures as "a surrender of parliamentary democracy to the coming dictatorship."

Mrs. Gandhi went on radio to defend her Draconian measures, telling the Indian people that they would benefit from the removal of constitutional restraints on her use of power.

All strikes and picketing were banned as essential to the "fight against Fascism." Formerly when labor disputes threatened, many employers had agreed to arbitration. Now they had only to send for the police.

New decrees forbade Indians to speak against the government, or gather in groups of five or more to express grievances. Permits were required to travel or live in another part of India. People could no longer choose their own trades or occupations. And they could be held in jail without trial for up to two years, without having to be told why.

At trials, witnesses for the defense often failed to testify, hiding out of fear. Others were not allowed to appear because they were in jail themselves.

State governments that disapproved of what Mrs. Gandhi was doing did not long survive. The "President's Rule" was used to "dismiss" such governments and replace them with rulers handpicked by Delhi.

Many Indians defied Mrs. Gandhi's dictatorship. In the state of Gujarat demonstrators lit bonfires of protest. At the University College of Trivandrum students went on strike, boycotting classes. In Poona anti-government riots broke out. An attempt was made in Bombay to mount a general strike, but the effort failed.

Hoping to make her dictatorship more popular, Mrs. Gandhi ordered raids on the shops of some profiteers, which drove down the prices of staples. At the same time she enlisted the cooperation of industrialists by relaxing price controls to afford them higher profits. She promised land distribution to peasants, irrigation to landowners, lower taxes to the middle classes.

At the urging of her son Sanjay, she launched an aggressive birth control program in 1976 to cut down India's teeming population. The exploding birthrate contributed heavily to the nation's poverty and misery, but parents resisted planned parenthood because of the high death rate for children. They wanted many sons in order to ensure that some would survive to help them in the fields and to look after them in old age.

Village and city officials all over India were enlisted in a crash program of vasectomy, or male sterilization. Almost all men who had over three children were ordered to submit to this operation. Penalties for refusing included a fine and imprisonment, or loss of government jobs, housing, and pensions.

Sidewalk sterilization clinics were set up under tents. Men were swept up nightly by the tens of thousands and delivered to the tents. The campaign was so helter-skelter that many youths who were not even married were sterilized. In 1976 over 7 million sterilizations were reported.

One forty-five-year-old cobbler who had been forcibly sterilized declared, "They humiliated me and made me sick. After the operation there was infection and pain. I couldn't work and I had to borrow money." Some deaths occurred.

Male teachers were told not to report for work unless they had a certificate of sterilization. Three movie houses in New Delhi were closed for "sanitary violations" and reopened only when the owner had all his employees sterilized.

Muslims fiercely resented the vasectomy campaign, considering it a Hindu trick to reduce the Muslim population.

This resentment flared into open rebellion in April 1976. A vasectomy task force sent by Sanjay Gandhi descended upon a slum quarter near the Turkman Gate in Old Delhi. Sanjay, who was also running a slum clearance program, sought to get both jobs done simultaneously by including bulldozers in the task force.

Some of Sanjay's men rounded up male slum dwellers and rushed them off to vasectomy tents. Others collected families and transported them to a new development on the edge of the city, as bulldozers began to destroy their homes. Bewildered Muslims did not know what was happening. Old men and Muslim priests ran through the slum quarter shouting that the Hindus were destroying Muslim homes, seizing the women, emasculating the men, and putting them in prison camps.

"Throw the Hindu infidels back into the vans!" one Muslim yelled. "Guard your women and children in the name of Allah and defend your religion!"

Women and children barricaded themselves in their hovels. A furious mob of Muslim men hurled rocks, bricks, and Molotov cocktails at the interlopers. Sanjay summoned police, who charged the crowd, firing. The riot went on for hours. Before it was over fifty Muslims lay dead in the streets, and hundreds more had been injured.

The surviving slum dwellers were forced into vans at gunpoint and driven off to the new settlement. This proved to be empty farmland fenced with barbed wire. Each family received twenty-five square yards of land and bricks to build themselves shelters. They were issued ration cards for food, renewable only upon presentation of sterilization certificates.

The Turkman Gate riot was only one of many outbreaks that erupted across India.

More and more dissenters went underground to challenge the Gandhi dictatorship. In the state of Bihar they fought running gun battles with police. A Calcutta lawyer declared, "The thing that amazes me is that the shooting sometimes goes on all day. There are a lot more guns out there than the Government cares to admit!"

One letter smuggled out of Calcutta told sympathizers in the West, "There are thousands of us now working underground who would shed their last drop of blood for restoring our liberty and safety."

Foreign correspondents who tried to learn what was going on were shadowed by government spies. Their mail was opened, their hotel rooms broken into, and their belongings rifled.

Mrs. Gandhi exhorted the Indian people not to complain or listen to complaints. Billboards, buses, trucks, and buildings were plastered with slogans: WORK MORE, TALK LESS . . . RUMOR-MONGERS ARE THE NATION'S WORST ENEMY.

Police raids on universities swept suspected dissidents to prison. Faculty members carefully referred to jailed colleagues as "temporarily out of station." Delegations of teachers and students, workers, writers, businessmen, and trade unionists were ordered to appear at Mrs. Gandhi's residence to congratulate her on her emergency program.

Newspapers dutifully praised her crackdown on black-marketeering and corruption, and her slowing of inflation. Companies seeking government favors ran full-page ads praising the regime's achievements. One English language weekly, *Opinion*, refused to join the sycophantic chorus, declaring, "The current Indira regime . . . was born through lies, nurtured by lies, and flourishes by lies." The paper was shut down.

Most educated Indians knew the truth, despite the censorship. But they felt helpless to do anything about it, and ashamed of their ineptitude.

"Before, when I went to Singapore or Bangkok, I was proud of being an Indian," declared one New Delhi businessman. "I could hold my head up and say, 'Yes, we are poor, but by God we are free.' Now, we are becoming a dictatorship like all the rest of them and are still poor besides."

Just before the government's mandate from Parliament ran out in March 1976, Parliament obliged Mrs. Gandhi by postponing elections for another year. In November 1976 Parliament granted another postponement. At this, a new civil disobedience campaign began on November 14, Nehru's birthday.

Every day prominent citizens led street demonstrations. Batches of peaceful protesters offered themselves up for arrest. Police imprisoned them as inconspicuously as possible. Tight censorship made certain that no report of the demonstrations appeared in any Indian paper or on any radio broadcast.

But the pressure of the daily demonstrations forced Mrs. Gandhi to change her mind. In January 1977 she announced that she was dissolving Parliament, and that new elections would be held on March 16. The demonstrations, having achieved their purpose, were terminated.

Mrs. Gandhi's decision to risk elections was also influenced by other factors. She was getting highly unfavorable headlines in the United States, where her first cousin, Nayantara Sahgal, was testifying about her dictatorship at a congressional hearing. An election victory, Indira Gandhi hoped, would convince Americans that she was the free choice of a majority of the Indian people.

Mrs. Gandhi was also being made to look bad by her

arch rival, Prime Minister Zulfikar Ali Bhutto of Pakistan.
Announcing that he would hold elections in March, Bhutto
called his dictatorship "South Asia's only democracy," a jape
at Mrs. Gandhi's regime.

An excellent grain harvest made Mrs. Gandhi confident
that Indian voters would "vote their bellies" in her favor.
Moreover, she had effectively disrupted her political opposition by jailing most of its leaders. Even if she released some
in January to participate in the elections, they would have
less than two months to organize a campaign, and would
probably end up quarreling with each other—as usual.

An election victory would also give Mrs. Gandhi total
control of the Congress party, with the power to eliminate or
ignore members opposed to her. Finally, she wanted Sanjay
to win a seat in Parliament, so that she could groom him as
her successor.

To avoid being accused of holding unfree elections, she
announced a relaxation of the emergency regulations under
which Indians had been living for eighteen months. Giving
the impression that she would release all political prisoners
from detention, she actually freed only the best known.

Tens of thousands of lesser known state and district political workers remained locked up. Many went on a hunger
strike. George Fernandes, one of those kept in jail, urged
those freed to boycott Mrs. Gandhi's "sham elections."

Her chief rival, Morarji Desai, and others quickly organized four major opposition parties into the new national Janata party. With practically no funds or effective organization,
it faced a seemingly impossible task. Could it get its message
across to 320 million voters, scattered over half a million villages, in barely two months?

Janata leaders called a giant political rally in Delhi.

"You have found out what kind of people rule this country," Desai told the 70,000 people who attended. "It is as important to keep our freedom secure from this type of government as to keep it in the face of a foreign threat."

He drew a roar of approval when he denounced the government for having "vasectomized" democracy.

Although censorship had technically ended, laws still prohibited the press from "exciting disaffection" or "defaming" government leaders. Newspapers were careful to print nothing that might earn their editors a jail sentence.

From Dallas, Mrs. Gandhi's cousin Nayantara Sahgal charged, "The elections are useless unless they are held in a free society." She accused her cousin Indira of simply trying to "cloak herself in the mantle of political legitimacy."

Another relative who openly opposed Mrs. Gandhi was her aunt, Nehru's sister Vijaya Laksmi Pandit. A former Indian ambassador, she had also been president of the United Nations General Assembly. Mrs. Pandit told reporters that although she loved Indira dearly, she would speak out candidly in the campaign "in order that democracy can be put back on the rails in this country." She denounced Mrs. Gandhi's rule as one "when the Emergency is the law of the land and one by one all the freedoms . . . are suffocated."

Jaya Prakash Narayan, freed and dying, warned the Indian people that "This is the last chance. If you falter now, nineteen months of tyranny shall become years of terror."

Mrs. Gandhi was stunned when her food and agriculture minister, Jagjivan Ram, suddenly resigned from her Cabinet and the Congress party to organize a new party against her. His defection was a stunning blow because he was the acknowledged leader of India's 85 million untouchables.

In the short time they had for campaigning, rightists, leftists, and centrists in the Janata party united around their one common bond—the determination to end dictatorship. They did not, as in the past, split their vote by running candidates against each other. All contests were between Mrs. Gandhi's Congress party and the Janata or one of the other opposition parties.

Mrs. Gandhi campaigned for almost a month, speaking in all 22 states to 224 public meetings. She made certain that food was widely distributed in states suffering food shortages.

Warning Indians that her opponents would lead the country to "indiscipline, chaos and anarchy," she demanded, "How can anyone trust them?"

To make up for meager coverage in the captive press, the Janata conducted an intensive word-of-mouth campaign in the villages. The news flashed through rural India about the jailing of such venerated elders as Desai and Narayan; about the power over Indians' lives wielded by Mrs. Gandhi's unelected son Sanjay; about the force used in the vasectomy and slum clearance campaigns. Millions of Indians who had been kept from hearing about these events by censorship were outraged.

The American journal, the *Nation*, reported that in the last days of the campaign Mrs. Gandhi tried unsuccessfully to get Indian army contingents stationed in key states, either to rig the elections or to overturn the results and declare martial law if she lost.

The poor of India turned out at the polls in long lines. Not all were clear about the issue of democracy versus dictatorship. But most were fed up with Mrs. Gandhi's centralized, authoritarian emergency state which ignored individual rights. They wanted an end to arbitrary programs carried out blindly, often cruelly and stupidly, by local bureaucrats.

When the polls closed, a vote count revealed that a record 60 percent of the electorate had participated. The Janata party had received 43 percent of the ballots, the Congress party only 35 percent, and other parties had split the rest.

To add to Mrs. Gandhi's humiliation, she was overwhelmingly defeated in her home constituency by her foe Raj Narain. Even George Fernandes, jailed and awaiting trial on charges of criminal conspiracy to overthrow the government, had won his election bid. Every one of Mrs. Gandhi's ministers and advisers went down to defeat in their own campaigns for reelection to Parliament. Sanjay lost by a huge margin.

Stunned, Mrs. Gandhi told the nation, "The collective judgment of the people must be respected. My colleagues and I accept their verdict unreservedly and in a spirit of humility."

The rule of the Congress party and the power of Mrs. Gandhi's family—which had directed it for almost the entire thirty years since India's independence—came to an end.

Having no choice, Mrs. Gandhi now canceled the emergency she had imposed in June 1975, restored civil liberties, abolished censorship, and freed thousands of political prisoners. Then she resigned. Morarji Desai, the new prime minister, promised the people immediate restoration of democracy.

"You need not fear this government as you had feared all those months," he told a cheering mass rally. "We are your servants and not your masters."

Jubilant celebrations throughout India were reminiscent of Independence Day. In New Delhi cheering throngs raced through the streets. Happy Indian artists drew blood from themselves with which they painted portraits of the victors in the election.

By November, however, Mrs. Gandhi's supporters had

regrouped, and in her home district she won a seat in Parliament. Desai's Janata party promptly took action to expel her by having the lower chamber of the Parliament vote her guilty of interfering with a legislative probe of her son Sanjay's auto business. She was imprisoned until the end of the session.

"The punishment is lenient," said Desai, "considering the enormity of the crime. No one can claim to be above the law."

Mrs. Gandhi's imprisonment, however, won sympathy for her, made her a martyr in the eyes of many, and touched off riots in a number of Indian cities. In the violence sixteen persons died, hundreds were injured, buses were burned, and trains derailed. Over 120,000 Gandhi supporters were arrested and many of them voluntarily climbed into police wagons to demonstrate passive resistance. Two armed supporters hijacked an Indian airliner, demanding Mrs. Gandhi's release.

She was finally released after a week in prison.

Too late Mrs. Gandhi had recognized the basic mistake that had caused her fall from power. She had failed to perceive the depth of the Indian people's commitment to personal freedom. Indians preferred the inefficiency of democracy to the supposed benefits of discipline under authoritarian rule.

Kuldip Nayar, editor of the *Indian Express*, who spent two months in jail for protesting Mrs. Gandhi's censorship, declared, "I criticized the chaos before the emergency like any other thinking man. But it is possible to have liberty and bread in India without resorting to authoritarian rule. You don't use a hammer to kill a fly. Mrs. Gandhi forgot certain basic democratic principles, and that was her mistake."

Mrs. Gandhi's final mistake was to imagine that she could

win an honest election after she had destroyed human rights. Every voter who seized the chance to throw Mrs. Gandhi out of power legally was telling her defiantly, "You can't do that to me!"

Ironically, however, the new Indian coalition government proved weak and ineffective in coping with India's difficult economic problems. In the January 1980 election, Indira Gandhi campaigned again, promising to reduce food prices. The Indian people, weary of a runaway inflation, chose to forget the abuses of her twenty-one month emergency and gave her a second chance to solve India's problems democratically as prime minister. In an interview with *Newsweek* she declared of her earlier rule, "if anyone was hurt in any way, well, I regret it. . . . Perhaps we should have lifted it [the emergency decree after the first year]. . . . I got tempted by the fact that the economy had improved, and I thought that if I could once put it on a sound basis, then it [continuation of the state of emergency] would not matter." She promised, now, that India would continue to operate as a democracy.

So perhaps she had, indeed, learned the lesson the Indian people had taught her in 1977.

12

TORCH
IN THE SOVIET DARK

Sakharov
and the Russian Resistance

Weary Muscovites Andrei D. Sakharov and his wife Yelena arrived in Omsk, Siberia, to attend a political trial. A Crimean Tatar nationalist was being charged with "slandering the state." When the Sakharovs tried to enter the courtroom on the morning the trial opened, they were stopped by Soviet police and told that no seats were available. Sakharov quietly pointed to empty seats and insisted on the right to occupy them.

He and his wife were arrested and taken to police headquarters. Sakharov won their release by signing a police "confession" that he had been "disorderly." He and his wife returned to court next day, once more seeking to be seated as spectators. They were arrested again. This time Yelena Sakharov was flung down a flight of stairs by plainclothes policemen.

Many of his colleagues considered Andrei Sakharov, winner of the 1975 Nobel Peace Prize, a foolhardy eccentric. No one else took so seriously Article 111 of the Soviet constitution, which specified, "In all Courts of the U.S.S.R. cases are heard in public." Often denied admission to political trials, Sakharov stood a lonely vigil outside courtrooms barred to him, a tall unpretentious figure with sad, gentle eyes.

His presence at the trials was a constant thorn in the Kremlin's side, a symbol of the struggle of Soviet dissidents for human rights. The government denounced him as a traitorous ingrate who had received its highest awards, only to "betray" Communism. Sometimes officials called him a madman.

Born in Moscow in 1921, Sakharov was brought up by his father, a physics teacher, with respect for scientific integrity. When Stalin took over from Lenin, Soviet scientists, artists, and writers were ordered to devote all their efforts to advancing government goals. Pure science, art for art's sake, and experimental writing were labeled "bourgeois deviations" and condemned as cultural crimes. Soviet intellectuals who refused to obey Stalin's commands, or who dared criticize the government, were severely punished.

At an early age Sakharov proved his brilliance as a theoretical physicist. He won great prestige by helping to develop the Soviet Union's hydrogen bomb. "When I began working on this terrible weapon," he said later, "I felt subjectively that I was working for peace, that my work would help foster a balance of power. . . . It was a natural point of view shared by many of us, especially since we actually had no choice in the matter."

At thirty-two he became the youngest full member ever admitted into the Academy of Sciences. He was given top-level security clearance, with bodyguards to protect him wherever he went. Awarded the Stalin Prize, he also won the country's highest civilian medal, the Order of the Red Banner of Labor, three times. With these honors went a suburban dacha and a salary of $26,500 a year. Living simply, he accumulated $153,000.

Then, feeling guilty over his role in developing the hydrogen bomb, he donated his savings to cancer research.

In 1958 Sakharov, worried about the danger of contamination from nuclear fallout, protested to Nikita Khrushchev, the new Communist boss in the Kremlin, against Soviet tests of the H-bomb in the atmosphere. Khrushchev refused to call off the tests. "Sakharov is a good scientist," he declared. "But he is trying to teach us politics, and we know politics better than he does." Khrushchev used subtler tactics than Stalin had in dealing with dissidents.

Stalin's critics and those Stalin suspected of opposing him had been ruthlessly purged by execution and exile to Siberian prison camps. Author Alexander Solzhenitsyn spent eight years in the Soviet labor camp system for writing a friend letters critical of the dictator. Even after Stalin's death in 1953, intellectuals were afraid to protest his policies.

In February 1956, however, his successor Nikita Khrushchev had startled the world by a bitter denunciation of Stalin's crimes. Only then did the floodgates open. "De-Stalinization" brought liberalization of Soviet civil and criminal codes, and some freedom to dissent. Encouraged, Russian intellectuals began demanding freedom of speech, press, and assembly. Among those who spoke out were many of the most talented Soviet writers and scientists. Khrushchev had a more devious way of dealing with dissent.

In 1961 when Major General Pyotr Grigorenko publicly criticized Khrushchev's failure to restore human rights, KGB secret police hustled him off to Moscow's Serbsky Institute of Forensic Psychiatry. Here he was diagnosed as "paranoid" and confined to a mental hospital. Such confinement became the new pattern of punishment for prominent dissenters.

Once political prisoners were locked up in mental institutions, they lost all political rights. Dulled by heavy doses of tranquilizers, they were pressured to recant their anti-government views in order to regain their freedom.

At a White House press conference President Dwight D. Eisenhower was asked what he had done about the denial of human rights in the Soviet Union.

"Well, not much," he replied. "What can we do except deplore it? We can't impose our human rights standards on another country. Right now, we're trying to avoid another war. Nagging the Soviets about the lack of freedom in their country would contribute nothing to that effort."

Sakharov irritated Khrushchev by persistently warning him of the dangers of nuclear contamination, and urging him to cancel the big new atmospheric bomb test scheduled for September 1962. Although Sakharov was privately assured that it would be canceled, the test took place.

"I had an awful sense of powerlessness," the chagrined scientist said later. "I could not stop something I knew was wrong and unnecessary. After that, I felt myself another man. I broke with my surroundings. It was a basic break. After that, I understood there was no point in arguing."

He nevertheless continued to press for a limited ban on nuclear testing in air, sea, and space. In 1963 the Soviet Union signed a partial test ban treaty with the United States.

Sakharov next angered Khrushchev by rallying scientific colleagues to reject a Khrushchev candidate for election to the Academy of Sciences. The candidate, a biologist, had asserted the right of the state to control scientific investigation.

Khrushchev ordered the Soviet press to attack Sakharov as "a complete ignoramus" on biology. In a bold reply to Khrushchev, Sakharov upheld the right of scientific freedom.

The Soviet party leader angrily ordered the secret police to get something on Sakharov, "to teach him a lesson."

But before this order could be carried out, Khrushchev fell from power and was replaced in 1964 by Leonid Brezhnev. Tougher on dissent than Khrushchev, Brezhnev ordered a crackdown on all crusaders for human rights. Writers were arrested and jailed for sending censored manuscripts abroad for publication. Brezhnev even tried to rehabilitate the discredited image of Stalin as a hero of Soviet history.

Sakharov joined with twenty-four other leading Soviet figures to denounce the rehabilitation plan in an open letter. This defiance led Brezhnev to purge 1,500 Soviet intellectuals, whom he considered to be the backbone of the Russian resistance movement.

The purge began with the arrest of Yuri Galanskov and three other prominent journalists for editing an underground magazine. Sympathizers who organized a protest demonstration in Pushkin Square were also arrested.

Sakharov denounced the "crippling censorship of Soviet political and artistic literature." KGB Chief Vladimir Semichastny wanted to arrest him for heading a "secret anti-communist front" of Soviet intellectuals. But with the fiftieth anniversary of the Soviet Revolution impending, Brezhnev was anxious to avoid unfavorable international publicity. The KGB was ordered to leave Sakharov alone.

Smaller fry were prosecuted instead, as a warning to all intellectuals. In 1966 the trial and conviction of two talented young writers, Andrei Sinyavsky and Yuri Daniel, triggered a concerned protest movement. Sakharov and other dissidents demanded that the government respect the right to speak, write, and publish freely. They also protested illegal trials, censorship, the persecution of Jews and other minorities, the curtailment of religious freedom, and the ban on exchanging scientific information and visits with other countries.

Brezhnev found himself in a dilemma. Many of the dissenters were physicists and biologists who occupied high places in the Soviet regime, and were considered, like Sakharov, indispensable. (It was easier to do without writers than scientists.) A few minor scientists were exiled or imprisoned, but the major figures received only stern reprimands and warnings.

On December 5, 1966, Sakharov committed his first act of public dissent. He took part in a one-minute vigil in Pushkin Square organized by Vladimir Bukovsky to commemorate International Human Rights Day. Protesting the prosecution of Galanskov, Daniel, and other dissidents, the demonstrators demanded amelioration of the harsh conditions political prisoners suffered in the work camps of Siberia.

Bukovsky and others were seized and jailed.

Early in 1967 Sakharov wrote a 10,000 word essay, "Progress, Coexistence and Intellectual Freedom," which circulated in the underground newspaper, *Samizdat*. In it he urged an end to the arms race, and a cooperative struggle instead against world hunger. In the near future, Sakharov predicted, communism and capitalism would grow more like each other, with each becoming more humane. He criticized the Soviet system for its entrenched bureaucracy, which destroyed intellectual freedom through censorship and its appointment powers.

Published in the Western world in 1968, Sakharov's treatise created a sensation. The Kremlin could no longer ignore his defiance. Sakharov was fired from the nuclear program, and his security clearance was lifted. The word was passed that he was a pariah who no longer had any future in the Soviet Union. Any and all who associated with him risked great danger to themselves and to their careers.

Only Sakharov's international prestige and prominence as a symbol of dissent prevented his imprisonment.

Philip Handler, head of the U.S. National Academy of Science, wrote a letter to Mstislav Keldysh, head of the Soviet Academy of Sciences, warning, "Harassment or detention of Sakharov will have severe effects upon relationships between the scientific communities of the U.S.A. and U.S.S.R. and could vitiate our recent effort toward increasing scientific interchange and cooperation."

Significantly, the Soviet Academy did not expel Sakharov. In May 1969 he was rehired by the Lebedev Institute of Physics. However, his new post as a senior researcher represented a demotion. It also isolated him from the Soviet nuclear program he had helped to develop.

Unfazed, Sakharov donated most of his $440 monthly academy stipend to the families of imprisoned dissidents, and to a special fund he set up for their children.

At the trial of the Pushkin Square demonstrators, Vladimir Bukovsky defied the government after seven months in prison awaiting his day in court. "I absolutely do not repent of having organized the demonstration," he declared. "I believe it has done its job and, when I am free again, I shall organize other demonstrations!" He was sentenced to three years at forced labor and was followed to trial by Galanskov.

Sakharov joined over 700 scientists, artists, writers, sociologists, and engineers in signing petitions to the court demanding dismissal of the new "witch trial . . . no better than the celebrated trials of the 1930s which involved us in so much shame and blood that we still have not recovered."

But Galanskov was tried and convicted.

"Is it not a disgrace," Sakharov wrote in an underground pamphlet circulated in June 1968, "that Ginzburg, Galanskov and others were arrested, imprisoned for twelve months without trial and sentenced to five and seven years for activities which basically consisted in defending civil liberties?"

Signing petition after petition for the release of arrested intellectuals, Sakharov stood vigil at all their trials.

On August 25, 1968, Soviet troops invaded Czechoslovakia to oust the liberal Dubcek regime. Physics instructor Pavel Litvinov led a seven-person demonstration in Red Square to protest. KGB plainclothesmen swooped down upon them, tore the banners from their hands, and beat them savagely. All were arrested, and two were confined in mental institutions for "political insanity." At the trial of the other five, a crowd of almost 300 gathered outside the court to demonstrate opposition to the trial, despite roughing up by KGB operatives.

In the spring of 1970 biologist Zhores Medvedev denounced the government for censoring the mails to keep disapproving letters from Soviet scientists from reaching colleagues abroad. He blamed such censorship for the backward state of Soviet biology. In May 1970 Medvedev was arrested and placed in a mental institution.

Sakharov and other world-famous Soviet scientists raised a storm of protest. Author Solzhenitsyn called the imprisonment of Medvedev "spiritual murder" and "fiendish and prolonged torture." The outcry was so great and the international reverberations so loud that they forced Medvedev's release.

Leningrad mathematician Revolt Pimenov was arrested for "not living right"; he owned a collection of political books which he lent to friends. He told Party Secretary V. A. Medvedev, "We scientists have lost our sense of personal security. . . . The threat to personal security explains the studying of politics. All this began with the trials of the writers. . . . The violation of legal rights drew attention to them and aroused public concern."

"If you think that we'll let everyone say and write just what they like," replied Secretary Medvedev, "that will never happen. We still have enough power not to let people commit acts that will harm us. Never will there be any concessions at all in the sphere of ideology!" Pimenov was found guilty of "slandering the Soviet state," and exiled to Siberian prison camps for five years. This was the last straw for Sakharov.

In November 1970 he and physicists Valery Chalidze and Andrei Tverdokhlebov committed a daring act of defiance. They openly organized the Human Rights Committee to offer "constructive criticism" of the way the Soviet law was being used to crush personal freedom. They urged the Kremlin to turn "toward democracy and freedom . . . soon—before Russia suffers disaster."

The committee was open for membership to all but Communist party members. Solzhenitsyn was one of the first to join. Physicist Valentin Turchin and historian Roy Medvedev, twin brother of the biologist, followed suit.

To establish the committee's legality, Sakharov and his cofounders pointed to Paragraph 126 of the Soviet constitution, which "guaranteed [citizens] the right to unite in public organizations." The Communist party quickly made clear what it thought of Sakharov's committee.

"The opinion is sometimes heard that it is 'undemocratic' to use force against slanderers and provocateurs," declared Professor Grigory Deborin, "on the ground that such people are merely expressing 'different views'. . . . In many countries a person may be brought to court for defamation of another. The state has an equal right to defend itself against slander and baseless allegations which undermine its prestige."

Soon afterward Chalidze and Tverdokhlebov were fired from their posts. Under intense police surveillance, Chalidze accepted an invitation to visit the United States. The quick Soviet permission for the visit was explained by the Kremlin's revocation of Chalidze's citizenship while he was abroad.

Tension over human rights came to a fresh boil in 1970 when the Nobel Prize for Literature was awarded to Solzhenitsyn. The author was denied permission to go to Stockholm to receive the award. The Soviet press burst into an orchestrated condemnation of all Soviet writers whose works were smuggled out of the country and published abroad.

Sakharov told Western correspondents that so many intellectuals were active in the resistance because Socialism in Russia had proven a "grave disappointment." He said, "These people have true courage because, unlike me, the authorities have put them in prison. . . . Now that I live for my principles, I find many friends, warm friends. Not among the big people but little people, real people."

After his wife died in 1969, Sakharov married a pediatrician whom he met in 1970 while standing vigil at a political trial. Yelena Bonner was half-Jewish and half-Armenian; her father had been shot during the Stalinist purge, and her mother had been sentenced to eleven years in a Siberian concentration camp. Yelena quickly became Sakharov's partner in protest.

President Richard M. Nixon visited Moscow in May 1972 for a summit meeting with Brezhnev. They signed a treaty of détente that pledged the United States to "noninterference in internal affairs" of the Soviet Union.

"The authorities seem more impudent," Sakharov sighed afterward, "because they feel that with détente they can now ignore Western public opinion, which isn't going to be concerned with the plight of internal freedom in Russia."

At a press conference he urged the United States Congress to demand a price for agreeing to trade concessions for Russia—Soviet permission for all Russians who wanted to emigrate to do so. Sakharov warned against accepting détente on Soviet terms. "It would mean cultivating a closed country where anything that happens may be shielded from outside eyes," he said, "a country wearing a mask that hides its true face."

This comment was too much for the Kremlin. The Soviet press erupted with denunciations of Sakharov as a "despicable traitor to his country." *Kommunist*, the party's ideological journal, declared, "Academician Andrei Sakharov is allotted in the West the role of the fuse for the explosive device that the enemies of peace would like to put under the foundation of detente. . . . He slid into open slandering of socialism and . . . capitulation to bourgeois ideology and policy."

Sakharov still escaped arrest because any attempt to jail him would result in worldwide headlines, giving the Soviet Union a bad press and embarrassing Soviet diplomats by keeping Sakharov's name ringing in their ears as a martyr.

In 1972 Sakharov organized a protest demonstration at Moscow's Pushkin statue to mark the thirty-sixth anniversary of Constitution Day. Only twenty-five dissenters dared attend. They were far outnumbered by the police and secret agents present.

By the end of the year Sakharov was forced to admit that his Human Rights Committee had failed to force any significant change in Kremlin policy. "For us it is not a political struggle; it is a moral struggle," he explained. "We have to be true to ourselves."

The Soviet bureaucracy sought to discredit Sakharov by compelling many noted intellectuals to sign a statement suggesting that he belonged in a mental hospital. His dissent was treasonable, Russians were informed, because he was telling the world that the Soviet system was bad, and that the Americans should place restrictions on negotiations with Moscow.

Mstislav Keldysh, president of the Soviet Academy of Sciences, called Sakharov "politically blind."

Even his three children were turned against him and shunned contact with him. He responded with characteristic generosity, giving them his prestigious Moscow apartment and his dacha. His stepchildren, who supported him and Yelena, were fired from their jobs and barred from university admission. Yelena was denied medical care.

When Sakharov gave an interview suggesting that United States aid to Israel should match Soviet aid to the Arabs, two Black September terrorists called at his apartment and threatened to kill him if he made another statement. "We never give two warnings," they told him. Defying such personal threats, Sakharov pinned over his doorbell a cartoon of a bristling hedgehog labeled, "This is a hedgehog. Do not try to take him by hand."

"I have not been afraid personally for myself," Sakharov said. "I am mostly afraid of a kind of pressure being directed against my family, my wife's family and relatives."

A heart attack in the spring of 1975 did not stop Sakharov from continuing his struggle for human rights. From exile in the United States, journalist Vadim Belotserkovsky declared,

"Sakharov has saved the democratic movement in the Soviet Union. The whole movement might have died if it had been led only by people who lacked international prestige."

In August 1975 President Gerald Ford went to Helsinki to sign a new agreement on "European security" with the Soviet Union, Canada, and thirty-two other nations. The Helsinki accords required all signatories to "respect human rights and fundamental freedoms, including freedom of thought, conscience, religion or belief." Each nation subscribed to the precept that "No one must be subject to torture or to inhuman and humiliating treatment or punishment."

Few expected Moscow to give more than lip service to the human rights covenants of the agreement. But Sakharov and other Soviet dissidents viewed the accords as a new moral weapon in their struggle for freedom.

On October 20, 1975, acting on the recommendation of Solzhenitsyn, the Nobel Peace Prize committee awarded its prize to Sakharov for his tireless crusade for human rights. The committee hailed him as "a firm believer in the brotherhood of man, in genuine coexistence as the only way to save mankind."

Hearing the news, Sakharov said simply, "I hope this will help the political prisoners." The Kremlin furiously denounced the Nobel committee's award as an "open political ploy!" Tass, the Soviet news agency, branded Sakharov as an "anti-patriot who has taken a stand against his own country . . . and joined with the most reactionary, imperialist circles which are actively opposing the policy of peaceful coexistence."

In 1977 the president of the United States, Jimmy Carter, broke with the Eisenhower position by stating that his administration would stand firmly behind the principle of human rights for the citizens of every country in the world. The Kremlin smarted, especially when Carter indicated that he would ask Moscow for an accounting of its adherence to the Helsinki accords.

Sakharov wrote the president a letter that was delivered through a civil liberties lawyer who had visited Moscow. Sakharov told Carter that the suppression of human rights in the Soviet Union and East Europe was "a hard, almost unbearable situation." He declared, "Our and your duty is to fight for them."

Carter wrote directly to Sakharov, pledging that the issue of human rights would be "a central concern to my Administration." Brezhnev angrily warned the President that such "interference in Soviet affairs" could seriously jeopardize a new United States–Soviet Union agreement on nuclear arms limitation, and détente itself.

One day later the State Department issued a statement deploring the Soviet harassment of Sakharov, an "outspoken champion of human rights," and warning that attempts to intimidate him would be regarded as violations of "accepted international standards of human rights."

Anatoly Dobrynin, Soviet ambassador to the United States, phoned Secretary of State Cyrus Vance to protest this statement. With the President's approval, Vance subsequently declared, "We do not intend to be strident or polemical, but . . . we will from time to time comment when we see a threat to human rights, when we believe it constructive to do so."

No holiday greetings from abroad were allowed to reach Sakharov. His only foreign mail consisted of anonymous letters warning him against continuing his campaign for human rights. Significant photos of car crashes and corpses accompanied these warnings.

There was some evidence that the Carter administration's campaign was having an impact on Communist governments in East Europe, at least. The Communist party newspaper of Czechoslovakia ended a campaign of vilification against 320 dissidents who had signed a manifesto seeking to enforce human rights.

In Poland, party boss Edward Gierek went on TV to announce that many rioters in jail for protesting food price hikes would be released. In Yugoslavia the government agreed to consider a petition to grant passports to political dissidents.

In April 1977 Sakharov and a group of dissident Soviet scientists invited a team of Western scientists to a special seminar in Moscow, in keeping with provisions of the Helsinki accords. The Kremlin confined the meeting to the small three-room apartment of Jewish physicist Mark Azbel. Four American scientists were deliberately detained in Leningrad and at Moscow's airport, so that they missed the seminar. Three dissident scientists from Latvia, Estonia, and Lithuania were also prevented from flying to Moscow.

One Canadian and nine American scientists managed to attend the seminar. They were followed by KGB agents and photographed as they entered Azbel's apartment. Since a sound truck was parked outside, the scientists considered the apartment bugged. They confined any nonscientific remarks to notepaper or went for walks in a nearby park.

Despite these handicaps, the seminar was considered a success by both Soviet and American scientists. "This is really a step forward," said Professor William Glaberson of Rutgers University. "But we would all prefer to meet in Jerusalem."

To reinforce Sakharov's Human Rights Committee, Russian dissidents Aleksandr Ginzburg, Yuri Orlov, and Anatoly Shcharansky formed a new organization called Soviet

Groups to Promote the Observance of the Helsinki Agreement in the USSR. In 1977 the Soviet Politburo cracked down by arresting them and ten other founders.

When Shcharansky was indicted for treason, and faced possible execution by firing squad, the U.S. State Department announced that it was "deeply concerned" over this action against a dissenter "well known and respected in the United States for his efforts on behalf of human rights." *Izvestia* accused Scharansky of passing defense secrets to Unites States intelligence agencies through American correspondents and diplomats. But the Kremlin failed to bring him to trial for nine months, after which he was ordered detained without trial for another six months by a special decree of the Soviet Parliament.

In September 1977 the World Psychiatric Association condemned the Soviet Union for locking up in mental institutions over 200 Russians active in the human rights movement and diagnosing them as "sluggish schizophrenics." Andrei Snezhnevsky, head of the Soviet Institute of Psychiatry, denied that healthy persons were confined in psychiatric hospitals, and warned the association to "keep out of politics."

One month later Soviet author Georgyi Vladimov resigned from the Union of Soviet Writers, denouncing it as "a police body which utters hoarse urgings and threats" against writers who dare to defend human rights. "Do what you are best suited to do," he declared defiantly, "—suppress, persecute, detain. But without me." On December 10, 1977, he was arrested for publicly observing International Human Rights Day.

By 1978 Sakharov was the only unimprisoned leader left of the Human Rights Committee he had formed eight years earlier. His sense of humor still intact, he called himself "Andrei Blazhenny"—a Russian name connoting a saintly but mad Don Quixote. He refused to become cynical or disillusioned. "Were there no ideals," he declared, "there would be no hope. Then everything would be hopelessness, darkness—a blind alley."

Sakharov's crowded two-room, seventh floor apartment in Moscow remained the unofficial headquarters of the Soviet resistance movement. The phone rang constantly with calls from dissidents reporting their grievances. Each sought and received an endorsement of support from Sakharov. Others flocked to his apartment for advice, and often for sanctuary. Western reporters called to get his committee's news and appeals.

Many dissidents felt that Sakharov's crusade had forced some change on the Kremlin. "The KGB doesn't torture people any more to get confessions," a Moscow dissenter told a *Newsweek* reporter. "When they question you now, they never lay a hand on you. In fact, the prisoner even has the right to ask for a lunch break."

A Leningrad engineer told another *Newsweek* correspondent, "Twenty years ago I'd be sent to prison for talking with you. Ten years ago I'd still worry. Now I say what I like." But he prudently refused to be quoted by name.

Many intellectuals were made to understand that they'd be left alone as long as they didn't "make trouble." There was also a small increase in the number of Jews and other dissidents allowed to leave the Soviet Union.

"The important thing," pointed out Vernon Aspaturian, Penn State University specialist on Soviet affairs, "is that the dissidents are *still there*. Punishment . . . no longer means death or the kinds of incarceration that occurred under Stalin. It's a much different atmosphere altogether."

Malcolm Toon, former United States ambassador to the

Soviet Union, felt that the Carter administration's attempts to pressure the Soviet Union on human rights were well conceived.

"I think frankly the sort of posture that we've assumed in recent months is precisely the right one," he said in July 1977. "That is, to express our position with a good deal of candor and a good deal of sensitivity to other nations' concerns, to try to explain why it is we are so genuinely preoccupied with the cause of human rights, and explain as well that this policy is not aimed at any one country or at any one system. I think this is terribly important here in Moscow where the Soviets have a suspicion which is hard to dislodge, that the President's campaign is aimed at undermining Soviet power inside the Soviet Union and in Eastern Europe as well."

At the sixtieth anniversary of Communist power in Russia, Brezhnev told 6,000 Soviet and 104 foreign delegates in the Palace of Congresses, "Not everyone in the United States likes our way of doing things, and we, too, could say a great deal about what is going on in America."

But Sakharov's Human Rights Committee is beginning to embolden individual Russians to speak out and demonstrate on behalf of their grievances. In May 1978 when Vance flew to Moscow for the Strategic Arms Limitation Talks (SALT), Irina McClellan, a Russian woman married to an American professor, chained herself to the iron railing outside the United States embassy holding a poster that read: LET ME OUT TO MY HUSBAND.

In that same month the Kremlin, alarmed by its failure to silence the dissenters, toughened its policies. Dissident physicist Yuri Orlov was brought to trial for "slandering the Soviet state." Sakharov and his wife insisted upon being admitted to the trial, and were once again arrested for committing "insolent hooligan actions." They were released five hours later without formal charges.

When Richard Combs, first secretary of the United States embassy in Moscow, tried to get in to Orlov's trial, he was turned away, along with Western reporters. "Isn't this an open trial?" he demanded.

"Only for people with invitations," a policeman replied.

Orlov was found guilty and sentenced to seven years at hard labor, plus five years in exile, probably in Siberia.

Anatoly Shcharansky and Aleksandr Ginzburg—Orlov's fellow members of the Soviet Groups to Promote the Observance of the Helsinki Agreement in the Soviet Union—were held incommunicado for over a year. In July 1978, the Kremlin brought them to trial. Ginzburg was sentenced to eight years at hard labor for "anti-Soviet agitation and propaganda." Shcharansky was sentenced to thirteen years at hard labor for "espionage and anti-Soviet agitation and propaganda."

Sakharov bitterly denounced the trials as "pure sadism." They touched off a storm of international protests and demonstrations, and even the Communist parties of France and Italy joined in denouncing Moscow's brutal violation of human rights. On the other hand, the United States ambassador to the United Nations, Andrew Young, pointed out that there were "hundreds, perhaps thousands of people I would call political prisoners" locked up in America's jails.

This statement came at a time when President Carter was denouncing the Soviet trials, declaring, "We are all sobered by this reminder that, so late in the Twentieth century, a person can be sent to jail simply for asserting his basic human rights." He added, "Our voice will not be stilled as we consider these violations, and others around the world, of human rights." The president viewed the severe sentences of the dissidents as a personal rebuke to his human rights campaign. Furious at Ambassador Young for suggesting that the United States was just as repressive as the Soviet Union, Carter reprimanded Young and ordered him not to make any more statements that would embarrass the United States.

In March 1979 over 2,400 American scientists, including 13 Nobel Prize winners and 113 members of the United States' National Academy of Sciences, called for a boycott of scientific cooperation with the Soviet Union until Moscow released Orlov and Shcharansky from prison. And many United States Senators spoke out against ratifying the SALT II treaty.

Moscow decided that giving the Carter administration a human rights victory would encourage Senate ratification of the treaty and would, at the same time, rid the Soviet Union of some embarrassing prisoners. In May 1979 Aleksandr Ginzburg and four other Russian dissidents were released and allowed to leave the Soviet Union.

But in January 1980 the Kremlin decided to crack down on all remaining dissidents, to get them out of Moscow before the Olympics opened in the summer and thus deprive them of contact with Western journalists. Among those arrested was Sakharov, who was charged with "subversive work against the Soviet state," stripped of all his state awards, and sentenced to internal exile far from Moscow. He admitted being weary of the long struggle, but asked, "If not me, then who?"

The struggle will be long and difficult before the Soviet people can win the freedom to speak and write what they think, the freedom to read what they wish, the freedom to travel, the freedom to worship or not as they please.

But the Russian dissidents refuse to be silenced by prison, forced hospitalization, or exile.

"Even if what I am doing will not produce change in my lifetime," Sakharov has said, "it is not useless because it is a moral act. It is being true to what I believe in and must do."

13

THE PRICE OF LIBERTY

How Can We Protect Human Rights?

The decades of the 1960s and 1970s witnessed a tumultuous American struggle for human rights—notably, civil rights for blacks, and the right of citizens and draftees to protest and resist a war they considered unjust. Advances were made in securing these rights, but with a price paid in jail sentences, national turmoil, and deaths.

Other struggles for human rights in the United States are still going on. The right to read and see what we want is once more under attack. A Roper survey showed that almost one American in four—an increase of 66 percent over two years earlier—wants government censorship of programs shown on TV. Many communities are banning some magazines from newsstands, and seeking to put their publishers in jail.

Those who want censorship argue that TV programs and magazines with a high content of sex and violence are offensive to millions of Americans, who also believe them harmful to the young. Those who consider freedom from censorship guaranteed by the First Amendment reply that every adult should have the right to choose what he or she wishes to see or read, and that parents, not the government, should supervise what their children see and read.

The right to dissent, one of our most cherished human rights, is persistently challenged. Repeated attempts have been made to compel all Americans to conform to patriotic rituals such as standing to salute the flag and recite the Pledge of Allegiance, which contains a religious reference. Some citizens refuse to participate in the ceremony because they consider compulsory displays to patriotism a violation of personal freedom. Others are atheists or agnostics, or follow a religion which does not permit them to swear oaths of allegiance to any power but the God they worship.

Every time a case has been fought in the courts, the right of persons not to salute the flag or recite the Pledge of Allegiance has been upheld. Yet in June 1977, a sixteen-year-old, Newark girl, Deborah Lipp, was forced to conform to this patriotic ritual by her junior high school, with the backing of the New Jersey attorney general. Her parents went to court, supported by the American Civil Liberties Union (ACLU). U.S. District Court Judge H. Curtis Meanor confirmed Deborah's right not to participate in the ceremony, and issued an injunction forbidding the school to compel her to do so.

Outside the court, angry veterans' organizations distributed bumper stickers reading: "Send the Lipps back to Siberia." Deborah Lipp declared, "I am standing up for my personal beliefs. If I can't do that in New Jersey, then this state isn't as good as Siberia."

Freedom of thought is a human right that has to be rewon by every new generation. Over 200 years ago Thomas Jefferson said, "I have sworn upon the altar of God eternal hostility against every form of tyranny over the mind of man."

One of the passionate controversies of our day is whether

homosexuals should be accorded the same right as heterosexuals. In Dade County, Florida, singer Anita Bryant led a fight to repeal a statute giving equal rights to homosexuals. She argued that the Bible condemned homosexuality, and that homosexuals were unfit to be employed in schools. In a public vote on the issue, the Bryant forces won.

She then crusaded in other cities to oppose proposed laws or to overturn existing statutes protecting homosexuals' civil rights. Homosexuals organized their own campaigns to stop her, aided by heterosexuals concerned about the human rights issue.

Another important human rights struggle today is between those who support the right of a pregnant woman to decide whether to bear a child or have an abortion, and those who insist that the fetus has a right to life.

The National Organization for Women (NOW) supports the right to abortion. The Right to Life movement opposes it and is seeking a constitutional amendment to overturn the 1973 Supreme Court decision upholding abortion. Anti-abortionists argue that the act is nothing less than murder, and is a violation of the teachings of the Catholic church. Defenders of abortion argue that when over 2,000 unwanted children are born every day—many to the poor—every woman has the right to choose how many children she will have, and when.

A survey showed that 81 percent of all Americans and 76 percent of all Catholics support the position of Republican Senator Charles H. Percy, who opposed an anti-abortion law as denying women freedom of choice. "I personally view the central issue in the abortion controversy," he said, "to be the right of every woman to control her own reproductive life." His opponents argued that the unborn child's right to life is paramount.

Another vital human rights issue today concerns the question of building nuclear energy plants. Antinuclear forces insist that such plants pose a threat to the lives and health of everyone living nearby, as well as to the environment. Many Americans have joined organizations like New England's Clamshell Alliance and California's Abalone Alliance, which stage demonstrations against nuclear operations.

In 1977, on the thirty-second anniversary of the bombings of Hiroshima and Nagasaki, anti-nuclear forces staged civil disobedience actions in over 100 areas. Thousands of helium-filled balloons were released with messages reading: "This balloon symbolizes radiation. Releases of small amounts of radioactive material from nuclear facilities are routine. Did you realize they came this far?" Many activists staged sit-downs in front of the gates of reactor sites. Over 150 demonstrators were arrested.

In 1979 a serious accident at the nuclear reactor at Three Mile Island, Pennsylvania, frightened millions of Americans. The near-catastrophe caused a national uproar and a wave of new antinuclear demonstrations across the country. But millions of Americans argue that nuclear plants are necessary to supply the nation's future energy needs in a world of growing oil shortages and ever-higher energy prices.

In addition to the fights over human rights we face at home, we are confronted with the denial of human rights to the people of nondemocratic countries. Jimmy Carter was the first president since Woodrow Wilson to tackle the issue as an American cause.

"Sometimes people call me an idealist," Wilson declared. "Well, that is the way I know I am an American. America is the only idealistic nation in the world."

But international realities make it difficult to adopt a purist position, as Wilson discovered after World War I, when he was unable to prevent England and France from riding roughshod over the human rights of millions of others as they carved up the world for colonial spoils.

The great powers in the world today, those who can keep the world at peace or plunge it into nuclear war, are the United States, the Soviet Union, and the People's Republic of China. The Soviet and Chinese views of human rights and political freedom are far different from ours. This raises an important question: Do we have the moral right to impose our beliefs on them?

To what extent can we risk antagonizing them by denouncing their suppression of human rights? Could we alarm or anger them into freezing relations with the United States, or endangering world peace by stepping up the nuclear arms race? Is stopping political persecution a higher moral purpose than preventing the possible deaths of untold millions, including Americans, in a nuclear holocaust?

There are no easy answers to these dilemmas. Many professional diplomats in the United States State Department privately believe that moral principles and human rights should not be injected into the conduct of foreign policy. In their view, a "live and let live" doctrine, requiring us to stay out of the internal affairs of other nations, is the only practical basis on which necessary international accords could be reached.

"It can be argued that to boycott all countries that seemingly violate human rights is impossible," observed the *Nation*, "there being so many. That is true, but it ignores the symbolic effect of selective boycotts against the worst offenders." But the *London Times* pointed out that human rights cannot be the only goal of United States foreign policy —at least not in a world in which peace is literally a matter of survival.

Thus, the United States continued arming some despotic allies, Secretary of State Cyrus Vance told a congressional committee in 1978, because security considerations outweighed human rights values. As an example he cited the Philippines, which the State Department considers one of the worst violators of human rights, but which the United States needs for army and naval bases. Vance pointed out that stinging United States criticism of Uruguay and El Salvador had infuriated these dictatorships into spurning further American military aid.

Balancing U.S. aims, the American government recognized —without criticism—the People's Republic of China, where —for all that Communist government's economic, sociological, and medical achievements—there is no political freedom. In July 1977 Fan Yan-yen, a Chinese Air Force squadron leader and Communist party member, fled in his MIG-19 to Formosa.

"Life on the mainland is too hard," he told Formosan officials. "I defected because there are no human rights. There are many others waiting for their chance to escape."

Reporter Elizabeth Drew asked a United States foreign policy adviser why the federal government had failed to comment on the lack of human rights in China. The adviser replied, "Human rights, to be an effective political process, has to have . . . a constituency for it within the country, and the regime has to be at a stage where we could do something about it."

At the same time the "other China," Taiwan, proved just as insensitive, or more, to human rights. In January 1980, security police shut down all critical publications and rounded up and jailed sixty-five major opposition politicians who staged a Human Rights Rally.

Amnesty International found torture a common practice in many South and Latin American countries, where political opponents were jailed. This finding was confirmed by a 1978 U.S. State Department report on human rights in 115 countries that receive U.S. aid, or buy U.S. weapons—often for use against their own people.

In Uruguay army officers who called themselves "doctors" tortured prisoners, subjecting them to rape, whipping, electric shock, and having their fingernails pulled out.

In Paraguay young peasant girls aged eight to fourteen were purchased from poor parents and forced to provide sexual gratification to civilian and military authorities.

A CBS report in July 1977 revealed that in El Salvador, where 2 percent of the people are rich coffee growers and 98 percent are poverty-stricken peasants, foreign Catholic priests were arrested, tortured, and deported for teaching peasants their human rights.

In Nicaragua the Somoza family held power for over four decades by terror. An American-trained national guard has been used to beat, torture, and shoot peasants in order to seize their land, cattle, and women. Finally, in 1979 the country rose in revolt against the Somoza regime, and a democratic republic was established by the Sandinist rebels.

In Brazil, where a wealthy 3 percent of the people own 62 percent of the land, Dom Helder Camara, archbishop of Recife, supported opposition to the ruthless military junta in power as a "battle with the social disorder that keeps millions of human creatures living in sub-human conditions."

In Argentina army troops and police raided stores, farms, and buildings suspected as meeting places for government opponents. Between 1975 and 1977 over 3,000 people were killed in political violence.

One of the worst Latin American offenders against human rights was Chile. The ruling military junta, taking power in 1973, jailed and tortured thousands of democrats, liberals, labor leaders, and leftists. "Without torture," explained General Augusto Pinochet, head of the junta, "they don't sing."

In Paraguay General Alfredo Strassner's troops hunt local Ache Indians, selling them into slavery, to seize their lands, while semiofficial "death squads" terrorize the population by arbitrary arrest, torture, and executions.

The U.S. State Department report also found that in Saudi Arabia, arrested persons were beheaded or had their hands chopped off, and political parties and unions were prohibited. In Syria prisoners were tortured to secure confessions. In the Philippines President Ferdinand Marcos rigged elections and kept hundreds of political opponents in jail.

The report, published just before the fall of the Shah of Iran, noted that the Shah's police tortured, jailed, and killed thousands of dissenters. A revolution in 1979 forced the Shah to flee; his successor, the Ayatollah Khomeini, proved almost as repressive, executing without trial some 300 of the Shah's officials, and severely punishing Iranians who ignored strict Islamic religious precepts.

Our own country's stand on the abuse of human rights in other countries has been inconsistent. For example, almost all American administrations have been silent about such abuses in South America, even while giving aid to repressive dictatorships, because of extensive U.S. corporate investments in those countries.

For example, Americans were not informed when CIA machinations put the Shah of Iran in power, training and equipping his Savak, the secret police that tortured and killed thousands. This denial of human rights backfired badly on Washington when Khomeini held as hostages over fifty diplomatic personnel at the United States' embassy in Teheran, demanding the return of the Shah for punishment as the price of their release. Americans were outraged by this violation of human rights, and the World Court and the United Nations condemned it. But at the time these lines are written, Khomeini was ignoring all protests and U.S. economic pressures, blaming American support of the Shah for the crisis.

On the other hand, many American administrations have denounced the abuse of human rights in the Soviet Union and its East European satellites. Critics of this policy charge that it has only worsened East-West relations, without improving the human rights situation in the countries themselves.

In September 1977 Czech dissidents who distributed copies of a human rights manifesto signed by 800 people went to prison for three-and-a-half years. In 1979 Czech authorities arrested ten more leaders of this Charter 77 group.

In East Germany political prisoners went to jail for three years for criticizing government policy, seeking to exercise civil rights, or applying for permission to leave the country.

Violations of human rights continued in the Soviet Union. Even as Amnesty International won the Nobel Peace Prize in 1977, one Russian member of AI was punished for reporting human rights violations, and another was jailed.

Communist governments feel that they have to deal with dissent ruthlessly—stamping it out before it can spread, and inspiring fear in those tempted to join the voices of opposition.

In October 1977, at a European security conference in Belgrade, the United States sought to bring up violations of the human rights agreement the Russians had signed at Helsinki.

The Communists refused to allow witnesses to be produced to substantiate these charges.

The Soviet delegate mentioned human rights only once. He pointed out that Soviet disarmament proposals would guarantee the most important human right—"the fundamental human right to live." Accusing the United States of seeking to interfere in Soviet and East European internal affairs, he charged that American discrimination against blacks, Asians, and Chicanos violated the Helsinki accords.

Another Communist accusation against Washington came in 1979 from Fidel Castro, who pointed out that the United States, which supplied aid and arms to some of the world's most repressive dictatorships, refused to allow American pharmaceutical firms to do business with Cuba. "One of the most grotesque and miserable things is to deny a country even the right to obtain medicines," he declared. "I ask myself how can the embargo against Cuba be reconciled with these preachings about human rights."

Nevertheless, American protests against the violation of human rights have brought the issue out of the closet of diplomacy and made it of international importance. They have challenged the right of any government to mistreat its own citizens, or the citizens of another country. The solution to the problem, however, remains a long way off.

Notified that Amnesty International had won the Nobel Peace Prize, David Hawk, executive director of the United States division, declared, "We're honored and very moved at the prize. But we're not celebrating. The time when we're going to celebrate is when there is no more torture and atrocities committed by governments around the world."

That would first require an end to the suppression of free thought. AI reported in 1977 that one government had ordered all of its libraries to remove the books of 350 authors. It had fired 144 historians in universities and scientific institutes. All the children of the purged writers and historians had been expelled from school.

AI wages a persistent fight to free political prisoners it has "adopted." It organizes mail campaigns of protest designed to swamp and pester offending governments.

"Mail piles up," explained Sean MacBride, a founder of Amnesty International and former foreign minister of Ireland. "It's a nuisance. Sooner or later the matter is at Cabinet level and everyone is wondering whether the prisoner is worth all this trouble. The answer frequently is no."

The Swedish chairman of AI announced that the organization would use its $145,000 Nobel Prize money to expand its work in "countries where we are weak, including parts of Asia and Latin America where there is a great demand for our help."

Amnesty International's pressure was ineffective in restoring human rights in Communist Cambodia or Vietnam for huge numbers of people who had been on the losing side of the civil wars in those countries. Cambodia was estimated to have killed over a million people in cruel reconstruction measures. Vietnam kept thousands of political prisoners in so-called "reeducation centers," where they were subject to brutal conditions and torture, according to Amnesty International.

Singer Joan Baez, who had been one of the leaders of the protest movement against the war in Vietnam, felt compelled to speak out against the violation of the imprisoned Vietnamese's human rights. Organizing a Humanitas-International Human Rights Committee, she published an open letter, signed by 100 prominent persons, to protest to the Hanoi government which she had once championed.

Fleeing from the repression in Vietnam and Cambodia,

over 100,000 refugees—called "boat people" because they sailed away, bound for anywhere they could land—created an international human rights problem. The world was shocked in 1979 when the Malaysian government, overburdened with refugees, threatened to load 40,000 on ships and send them away, shooting any who tried to return.

The struggle for human rights is going on in almost every nondemocratic country in the world today, and in many which are democracies in name only.

Human rights are often granted or won only temporarily. Each generation produces new governments or administrations with different ideas of how much power to exercise over citizens' lives. More often than not, governments seek to reduce, not increase, personal freedoms. Governing is easier and produces quicker results with less opposition.

Only the vigilance of determined citizens united behind a bill of rights can keep their freedoms from being chipped away. It is one thing to be guaranteed human rights by law —as, for example, the Russians are in the Soviet constitution. It is something else to be able to enforce these rights when they are ignored or subverted.

As Americans, we have an obligation to pass the torch of liberty that has been handed down to us through twenty-five centuries by other lovers of freedom. But we cannot look only to our leaders to keep the torch lit for us. Leaders are often corrupted by power. Some trim their principles to prevailing winds, as a matter of political expediency.

Human rights can be preserved only by a people prepared to resist promptly and vigorously every effort made by government to whittle them away. We have had presidents and Congresses who paid lip service to human rights, but who were stamped ed into curbing them in the name of "national security." We will have them again.

In January 1975 a 753-page bill known as S.1 almost slipped unnoticed through Congress. Prepared by "law-and-order" zealots, it presumably "reformed" the criminal code. But within the fine print were provisions permitting unrestricted wiretapping, police entrapment, imprisonment for crossing a state line to lead or join a demonstration, and the death penalty for journalists who reported information from classified documents.

Liberals who waded through the bill raised an alarm, which was spread by the press. Law school professors at Harvard and Yale warned that the passage of S.1 would be "an unparalleled disaster for the system of individual rights in the United States." Its chagrined sponsors were forced to return the bill to committee to expunge its police state flavor.

We need to search for new ways to reconcile the need for individual freedom and the need for economic security. Both are valid human rights. It avails us little if we are politically free to speak, write, and read as we please—but also go hungry, freeze, or die from lack of medical care. On the other hand, few of us would settle for guaranteed jobs, food, homes, and a national health service if their price was political enslavement.

Are the two kinds of human rights incompatible? American pioneers had great freedom—even the freedom to kill Indians with impunity—with little government control of their lives. But they also had no security. Today Americans have more economic security. But they also have Social Security numbers, tax forms to fill out under penalty of jail, and other laws circumscribing their behavior. Many Americans chafe at "too much government" in their lives.

Is it inevitable that the more security we seek from our government, the more liberties we must surrender, and the greater the control government must have over us? Are the Soviet Union and the People's Republic of China evidence?

Today the struggle for human rights is economic as well as political. Perhaps we can learn better ways from the Russians and the Chinese to satisfy people's need for economic security. And perhaps these powers can learn from us how to satisfy people's need for political freedom. Then both kinds of human rights could be held in a fine balance, without the government becoming a tyranny.

One possible answer—not a perfect one, but one that seems to work reasonably well—may be found in the Scandinavian countries. The Swedes, for example, live better than almost everyone else in the world, including Americans. They enjoy a social democracy with total political freedom, as well as a welfare state which has no slums, full employment, free medicine, no hunger, splendid care for the aged, and an excellent free public education system. Perhaps we might ask members of Congress to send a study commission to Sweden to learn how they do it.

We also need to clarify our thinking about political violence as a tool for obtaining human rights. Most of us deplore the senseless terrorism that kidnaps innocent people, using them as hostages to force governments to make political concessions. Certainly there is no justification for such crimes in free countries, where dissidents have legitimate ways to pursue their grievances.

But what about the ETA terrorists in Spain under Franco, where the Basques were victims of government terror, denied any legitimate expression of protest? Or terrorists who operate against such brutal dictatorships as Uruguay,

Chile, Korea, and South Africa? Is selective terrorism against dictators, their security police, and their powerful supporters justified when an oppressed people has no other way to obtain its human rights?

The problem becomes even thornier when antagonists accuse each other of violating human rights. In 1978 both Israel and the Palestine Liberation Organization (PLO) were found guilty of committing atrocities against each other by impartial investigators. And during the civil war in Lebanon between Muslim and Christian Arabs, the Muslims accused the Christians of massacring seventy-five Muslim men, women, and children during the Israeli invasion, while the Christians accused the Muslims of tying a captured Christian leader to a jeep and dragging him for miles until he died.

Even as civilized a nation as Britain has been accused of human rights violations. The European Court of Human Rights, meeting in 1978 in Strasbourg, France, condemned the British government for letting its security forces use "inhuman and degrading" third-degree methods in interrogating suspected members of the Irish Republican Army seven years earlier.

Such brutality can never be justified by either governments or revolutionists. But few would deny oppressed peoples the right to revolt violently, as our founders did in 1776. The question arises, however, as to whether violence is the *best* method of winning human rights, even from a repressive government.

Often terrorism is counterproductive. The leaders of protest may be spotted and jailed or killed, leaving an oppressed people without dynamic leadership. Terrorism also frequently alienates and frightens the masses.

Propaganda is a slower but often more effective way to fight for human rights, because it gradually unites a whole people in support of the struggle. *Propaganda* is not a dirty word, although it is often used in that sense. Propaganda simply spreads an opinion or doctrine. Propaganda can be used in noble causes such as human rights, or in ignoble causes such as racial hatred.

Amnesty International's weapon is propaganda. AI educates the world about which countries are trampling on the citizens' human rights, and how. International protest is stirred, and governments are pressured into releasing political prisoners.

Guns alone are not the answer to securing human rights. In the long run we may do more for human rights if we help and support leaders of the caliber of Martin Luther King, Jr., Mahatma Gandhi, and Andrei Sakharov, and organizations like Amnesty International and the American Civil Liberties Union. We also have the powerful weapon of the vote to help the cause of human rights at home and abroad.

But even when we elect a president who expresses concern for human rights, we can't sit back and let others do it. Others may not. Influential blocs in Congress are often concerned far more with the wishes of powerful interests than with human rights. These lobbies may compel the lawmakers to compromise. The human right not to be exposed to nuclear radiation or smokestack pollution can be swept aside by the pressure of corporate lobbies.

Whenever human rights are endangered, self-preservation would indicate that we pitch in and join hands with neighbors in spreading the alarm. Once town meetings are filled with aroused citizens, action can be expected that will make the wishes of the people felt in the halls of Congress.

As Mazzini recognized, young people are the best hope the world has for achieving human rights. Many older people tend to be fatalistic, cynical, too engrossed in personal affairs, or too weary of the struggle against injustice.

Young people tend to be idealistic. Many are deeply outraged by violations of human rights, and they may have the energy, the courage, the spirit, and the enthusiasm to join crusades to make the world a better and fairer place.

There are many groups you can join to make your influence felt in this crusade. Chief among them are Amnesty International and the American Civil Liberties Union. But many young people are also flocking to anti-nuclear groups and groups to stop the agricultural use of certain chemical pesticides which poison not only consumers but farm workers. Still others are joining groups to stop the pollution of our air, water, and earth by corporations concerned only with profits, and not with the human rights violated in gaining profits.

You may want to consider starting your own group under such a name as "Youth For Human Rights," with the hope of linking up with other such groups to form a national organization. This is how SDS—the influential Students for a Democratic Society in the 1960s—began, but on a college level.

Your student group could rally for American ratification of the international human rights covenant, which many other nations have already signed and ratified.

Most Americans would probably be shocked to learn that our government, which is heard around the world as the champion of human rights, has so far ratified only five of the thirty-nine covenants in this vital international treaty.

The *Nation*'s Latin American correspondent, Penny Lernoux, points out that many countries will have difficulty in taking Washington's championship of human rights seriously as long as the U.S.A. fails to ratify the covenant. "Only the Americans," she points out wryly, "believe their own propaganda."

A spirited young people's crusade could demand action that speaks louder than words, focusing national attention on this issue. It could bring pressure on Washington to join with other nations of the world in branding any government which violates human rights an outlaw, unfit to participate in the international associations of nations, as was done when the United Nations condemned Iran for holding American hostages and the Soviet Union for invading Afghanistan.

You can also aid the worldwide struggle for human rights by publicizing and raising funds for the students of dictatorships who are fighting to overthrow their repressive governments. In the Nicaraguan revolution against Somoza, for example, hundreds of armed teen-age students manned guerrilla posts and held Somoza's national guardsmen at bay.

Even if your group can only send a public message of encouragement and support to teenagers in other lands who are fighting for human rights, your voices will inspire them with the knowledge that they have friends in the United States.

You can also keep the spirit of idealism burning brightly in the United States by writing letters to your local paper and to national magazines, deploring every violation or weakening of human rights at home and abroad.

Americans need to be reminded that the Bill of Rights is the foundation of our democracy—the document that made and keeps us a free people.

Autocratic leaders will always seek to curb human rights in order to gain greater control over citizens' lives and national affairs. The more these leaders succeed, the more the people will belong to the government.

People everywhere must demand their human rights, make them the law of the land in a constitution, and fight every effort by their government or courts to weaken them. Only then will the government truly belong to the people.

BIBLIOGRAPHY AND RECOMMENDED READING

*indicates recommended reading

1. NOTHING TO LOSE BUT YOUR CHAINS

Dudley, Donald R. *The Civilization of Rome.* New York: The New American Library, 1960.

*Fast, Howard. *Spartacus.* New York: Bantam Books, 1960.

Grant, Michael. *The World of Rome.* New York: The New American Library, 1960.

Household, H. W. *Rome: Republic and Empire.* London: J. M. Dent and Sons Ltd., 1936.

*Mannix, Daniel P. *Those About to Die.* New York: Ballantine Books, 1959.

Mommsen, Theodor. *The History of Rome.* New York: Philosophical Library, Inc., 1959.

Plutarch. *The Lives of the Noble Grecians and Romans.* New York: The Modern Library, 1932.

Rostovtzeff, M. *Rome.* New York: Oxford University Press, 1960.

2. No More, King John!

Holt, James C. *Magna Carta and the Idea of Liberty*. New York: John Wiley & Sons, Inc., 1972.

Pallister, Anne. *Magna Carta: the Heritage of Liberty*. Oxford: Clarendon Press, 1971.

Stenton, Doris M. *English Justice Between the Norman Conquest and the Great Charter*. Philadelphia: The American Philosophical Society, 1964.

*Swindler, William F. *Magna Carta: Legend and Legacy*. Indianapolis: The Bobbs-Merrill Company, Inc., 1965.

3. "Down With Traitors to the People!"

*Alderman, Clifford Lindsey. *Flame of Freedom*. New York: Julian Messner, 1969.

Dobson, R. B. *The Peasants' Revolt of 1381*. New York: St. Martin's Press, 1970.

Lindsay, Philip and Groves, Reg. *The Peasants' Revolt, 1381*. Westport, Conn.: Greenwood Press, Publishers, 1974.

*Oman, Charles. *The Great Revolt of 1381*. New York: Greenwood Press, Publishers, 1969.

4. Breaking the Shackles

Bailey, Norman A. *Latin America in World Politics*. New York: Walker and Company, 1967.

Clark, Gerald. *The Coming Explosion in Latin America.* New York: David McKay Company, Inc.

Ferguson, J. Halcro. *The Revolutions of Latin America.* London: Thames and Hudson, 1963.

Gunther, John. *Inside South America.* New York: Harper & Row, Publishers, 1966.

Nehemkis, Peter. *Latin America: Myth and Reality.* New York and Toronto: The New American Library, 1966.

*O'Leary, Daniel Florencio. *Bolivar and the War of Independence.* Austin: University of Texas Press, 1970.

*Waugh, Elizabeth. *Simon Bolivar.* New York: The Macmillan Company, 1942.

5. "WE DON'T LIKE YOUNG PEOPLE TO THINK"

*de Polnay, Peter. *Garibaldi.* London: Hollis & Carter, 1960.

Ergang, Robert. *Europe Since Waterloo.* Boston: D. C. Heath and Company, 1961.

Friedlander, Paul J. and Brooks, Joseph. *Italy.* New York: Simon and Schuster, 1955.

Grigson, Geoffrey and Gibbs-Smith, Charles Harvard, eds. *People.* New York: Hawthorn Books, Inc., Publishers.

*Hinkley, Edyth. *Mazzini.* London: George Allen & Unwin Ltd., 1924.

Langer, William L., ed. *Western Civilization.* New York: Harper & Row, Publishers, 1975.

May, Arthur J. *The Age of Metternich, 1814–1848.* New York: Holt, Rinehart and Winston, 1963.

*Salvemini, Gaetano. *Mazzini*. Stanford: Stanford University Press, 1957.

Walker, Mack, ed. *Metternich's Europe*. New York: Harper & Row, Publishers, 1968.

6. "WHO CARES WHETHER WE LIVE OR DIE?"

*Chesneaux, Jean. *The Chinese Labor Movement 1919–1927*. Stanford: Stanford University Press, 1968.

Franke, Wolfgang. *A Century of Chinese Revolution 1851–1949*. Columbia: University of South Carolina Press, 1970.

Kent, P. H. B. *The Twentieth Century in the Far East*. London: Edward Arnold & Co., 1937.

Robottom, John. *China In Revolution*. New York: McGraw-Hill Book Company, 1969.

Sheean, Vincent. *Personal History*. Boston: Houghton Mifflin Company, 1969.

Smedley, Agnes. *The Great Road*. New York: Monthly Review Press, 1956.

Snow, Edgar. *Red Star Over China*. New York: Grove Press, Inc., 1968.

Sun Yat-sen. *Memoirs of a Chinese Revolutionary*. Philadelphia: David McKay Company.

*Wales, Nym. *The Chinese Labor Movement*. New York: The John Day Company, 1945.

7. "JEWS? WHAT JEWS? I SEE ONLY DANISH CITIZENS!"

*Archer, Jules. *Resistance*. Philadelphia: Macrae Smith Company, 1973.

*Lampe, David. *The Danish Resistance.* New York: Ballantine Books, 1957.

*March, Tony, ed. *Darkness Over Europe.* Chicago: Rand McNally & Company, 1969.

*Shirer, William L. *The Rise and Fall of the Third Reich.* Greenwich, Conn.: Fawcett Publications, Inc., 1963.

8. THE BURNING SPEAR

*Archer, Jules. *African Firebrand.* New York: Julian Messner, 1969.

Burnett, Hugh, ed. *Face to Face.* New York: Stein and Day, Publishers, 1965.

Cox, Richard. *Kenyatta's Country.* New York, Washington: Frederick A. Praeger, Publishers, 1965.

*Kenyatta, Jomo. *Facing Mount Kenya.* New York: Vintage Books.

*Slater, Montague. *The Trial of Jomo Kenyatta.* London: Secker & Warburg, 1955.

9. "AVENGE THE DEAD!"

Ayling, S. E. *Portraits of Power.* New York: Barnes & Noble, Inc., 1963.

Blanshard, Paul. *Freedom and Catholic Power in Spain and Portugal.* Boston: Beacon Press, 1962.

Coles, S. F. A. *Franco of Spain.* London: Neville Spearman, 1955.

del Vayo, Julio Alvarez. *Give Me Combat.* Boston: Little, Brown and Company, 1973.

*Gallop, Rodney. *A Book of the Basques.* Reno, Nev.: University of Nevada Press, 1970.

*Knightley, Phillip. *The First Casualty.* New York: Harcourt Brace Jovanovich, 1975.

Payne, Robert. *The Civil War in Spain.* Greenwich, Conn.: Fawcett Publications, Inc., 1962.

Trythall, J. W. D. *El Caudillo.* New York: McGraw-Hill Book Company, 1970.

10. "FIDEL! FIDEL! FIDEL!"

*Archer, Jules, *Thorn In Our Flesh: Castro's Cuba.* New York: Cowles Book Company, Inc., 1970.

*Casuso, Teresa. *Cuba and Castro.* New York: Random House, 1961.

Draper, Theodore. *Castro's Revolution.* New York: Frederick A. Praeger, Publisher, 1962.

Dubois, Jules. *Fidel Castro.* Indianapolis: Bobbs-Merrill Company, Inc., 1959.

*Morray, J. P. *The Second Revolution in Cuba.* New York: Monthly Review Press, 1962.

Smith, Earl E. T. *The Fourth Floor.* New York: Random House, 1962.

Urrutia, Manuel. *Fidel Castro & Company, Inc.* New York: Frederick A. Praeger, Publisher, 1964.

*Zeitlin, Maurice, and Scheer, Robert. *Cuba: Tragedy in Our Hemisphere.* New York: Grove Press, Inc., 1963.

11. WHEN DEMOCRACY DIED IN INDIA

Bhargava, G. S. *After Nehru*. New York: Paragon Book Reprint Corp., 1966.

*Kachan, D. N. *Indira Gandhi: Three Years As Prime Minister*. Mystic, Conn.: Lawrence Verry, Inc., 1969.

*Kothari, Rajni. *Politics In India*. Boston: Little, Brown and Company, 1970.

12. TORCH IN THE SOVIET DARK.

*Bonavia, David. *Fat Sasha & the Urban Guerilla*. New York: Atheneum, 1973.

Constitution of the Union of Soviet Socialist Republics. Moscow: Foreign Languages Publishing House, 1962.

*Jacoby, Susan. *Moscow Conversations*. New York: Coward, McCann & Geoghegan, 1972.

*Levytsky, Boris. *The Uses of Terror*. New York: The Viking Press, 1971.

*Litvinov, Pavel. *The Trial of the Four*. New York: The Viking Press, 1971.

Rositzke, Harry. *The USSR Today*. New York: The John Day Company, 1973.

Also consulted for the chapters on the Basques, India, and the Soviet Union, and for the final chapter, were issues of *The Atlantic, The Australian Bulletin, Bulletin of Atomic Scientists, Business Week, Christian Century, Free China*

Weekly, London Times, The Nation, National Review, New Republic, New York, The New York Times, The New Yorker, Newsweek, The Progressive, San Francisco Chronicle, Santa Cruz Sentinel, Saturday Review/World, Society, Sunset, Time, U.S. News and World Report and *Variety.*

INDEX